A VERY SHORT, FAIRLY INTERESTING AND REASONABLY CHEAP BOOK ABOUT

HUMAN RESOURCE MANAGEMENT

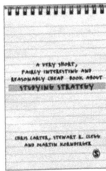
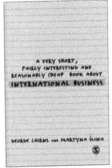

A VERY SHORT, FAIRLY INTERESTING AND REASONABLY CHEAP BOOK ABOUT

HUMAN RESOURCE MANAGEMENT

IRENA GRUGULIS

Los Angeles | London | New Delhi
Singapore | Washington DC | Melbourne

Los Angeles | London | New Delhi
Singapore | Washington DC | Melbourne

SAGE Publications Ltd
1 Oliver's Yard
55 City Road
London EC1Y 1SP

SAGE Publications Inc.
2455 Teller Road
Thousand Oaks, California 91320

SAGE Publications India Pvt Ltd
B 1/I 1 Mohan Cooperative Industrial Area
Mathura Road
New Delhi 110 044

SAGE Publications Asia-Pacific Pte Ltd
3 Church Street
#10-04 Samsung Hub
Singapore 049483

Editor: Kirsty Smy
Editorial assistant: Lyndsay Aitken
Production editor: Katie Forsythe
Copyeditor: Christine Bitten
Proofreader: Clare Weaver
Indexer: Gary Kirby
Marketing manager: Alison Borg
Cover design: Wendy Scott
Typeset by: C&M Digitals (P) Ltd, Chennai, India
Printed in the UK

The title for the 'Very Short, Fairly Interesting and
Reasonably Cheap Book about ... Series' was
devised by Chris Grey. His book, *A Very Short, Fairly
Interesting and Reasonably Cheap Book about
Studying Organisations*, was the founding title of this
series. Chris Grey asserts his right to be recognised
as founding editor of the Very Short, Fairly Interesting
and Reasonably Cheap Book about ... Series.

Library of Congress Control Number: 2016940135

British Library Cataloguing in Publication data

A catalogue record for this book is available from
the British Library

ISBN 978-1-4462-0080-3
ISBN 978-1-4462-0081-0 (pbk)

At SAGE we take sustainability seriously. Most of our products are printed in the UK using FSC papers and
boards. When we print overseas we ensure sustainable papers are used as measured by the PREPS grading
system. We undertake an annual audit to monitor our sustainability.

In loving memory of Janis Izidors Grugulis (1924–2010)
and Angharad Stella Grugulis, née Jones (1928–2015),
the best mum and dad in the word.

Contents

About the Author

Irena Grugulis is Professor of Work and Skills and Head of the Work and Employment Relations Division at Leeds University Business School. She is also an Associate Fellow and member of the Steering Group of the ESRC Centre for Skills, Knowledge and Organisational Performance at University of Oxford. She held an ESRC/AIM Services Fellowship, and served as Editor and Joint Editor-in-Chief of the journal *Work, Employment and Society* for seven years.

Her principal research interests lie in the (broadly constituted) area of skills, particularly the way that organisations attempt to shape their employees and the impact and implications of this for the employees themselves. The notion of a partial coincidence of interest between employer and employee is central to much industrial relations writing but has been largely neglected in the more prescriptive human resource development literature and she has tried to remedy this omission. Her research has been funded by the ESRC, EPSRC and EU. Recent research projects include an ethnographic study of work and skills in the computer games industry, a study of freelancers and small independent companies in UK film and TV production and research into work and skills in supermarkets.

She has published extensively including articles in *Organization Studies, Journal of Management Studies, British Journal of Industrial Relations* and *Work, Employment and Society*. She has also served on a range of government advisory boards including the UKCES Academic Advisory Board and the Leitch Review as well as acting as an advisor to the Singaporean government. Before settling down as a sensible academic, she worked in a range of jobs including translator, actor in a travelling theatre company and comedy writer for Radio 4. She thinks that she has the best job in the world, and she would like it even more if there were less of it to do.

Acknowledgements

This book has been made possible by many years teaching almost every HRM topic there is to cohort after cohort of students, and particularly by those students who managed to ask questions which made me think further about the subject area. This still happens and I hope it carries on happening for many more years. Thanks to all of you. I hope that, wherever you are, you are still asking questions that make people think.

It was written during a difficult time for me personally and thanks are due to more people than I could possibly name here. At work Tom Redman, Birgit Schyns and Miguel Martinez Lucio have been invaluable sources of support. Outside work Donna Rankine, Jules and Pete Chambers, Steve Elson, Leila Mottahedeh, David Ashton and (of course) James, Lewis, Will and Alfie have helped by offering time, friendship and holidays. Julie Greenwood, Julie Throup, Anwen Lewis and Karen Macmillan can always be depended on for coffee, conversation and lots more. Thanks too to everyone in my Tuesday evening group for listening with such patience. I must also mention my family, Bronwen Jones, Lin, Shaun, Danny, Keeley and Tegan Green, Doreen Jones, Glyn Jones and the (growing) clan, and Alwyn and Karen Hill who (amazingly) still write postcards.

Last, but never least, lots of love to my daughter Zinta. Perhaps the next book will be a proper adventure story.

Should You Buy This Book?

Definitely. Please do. This book is primarily intended for university students studying management or HRM at postgraduate or undergraduate level. It's also for people who aren't on formal courses but are just interested in the way organisations operate or what happens at work and who are fed up with the sort of happy clappy self-help books that assume that all society's ills can be cured if you smile manically.

You should buy this book if:

- You want to read something that is really short
- You are interested in what people (really) do at work and how they are managed
- You are particularly interested in what happens when it all goes wrong
- You are interested in HRM
- You'd like to find out about one of the topics in this book
- You want to impress your lecturer by doing extra reading, but don't want to do too much work
- You don't want to spend too much money

You should not buy this book if:

- You want a long textbook
- You want to know about one of the topics this book does not cover
- You want lists of the absolutely right answer in every situation that you can just learn by rote
- You want a 'how to' guide that ignores the fact that most people are human
- You think that all leaders are great, that organisational initiatives only go well, and you really don't want this view challenged
- You haven't got the money (please feel free to borrow the book from the library – that's what they are for)

If you do buy this book and want to come back on anything in it, you can e-mail me on i.grugulis@leeds.ac.uk.

Human Resource Management

Work is important. Not only does it consume a large part of our adult lives, but also the jobs we hold influence the people who we meet, where we live, what hobbies we get to enjoy, the number of children we have (seriously!) and the social class that sociologists ascribe to us. So a book which looks at what people do at work, what is done to them and what happens as a result is itself pretty important.

That is what this book is about. It's called Human Resource Management (or HRM) because that is the acronym which is currently popular but that does not mean that this book will limit its perspective to management, or even that it takes the management perspective. An essential feature of this series is that the books published in it are critical; which is great because frankly, when you look at HRM it is the critical aspects that are most interesting. Of course this book will deal with some of the key employment practices like strategy, team-working, empowerment, skills and training and pay, among others, but it will not insult your intelligence by trying to convince you that any or all of these are the solution to every organisational ill, nor that these practices always work, no matter how unpropitious the conditions, nor that they make workers happy. HR practices do work sometimes. In some firms. With some people. But not all the time with everyone. And finding the reasons for those differences or explaining why practices *don't* work is far more constructive than pretending that they do. This book will also deal with the dark side of HRM: redundancies and discrimination, without euphemisms and without pretending that they are aberrations, one-off exceptions, unlikely to be repeated or soon to be outgrown, because very often they aren't.

This means that this book is not one of the Happy HRM books that fill the bestseller shelves in airports and railway stations, and which claim to offer, in evangelically couched rhetoric, transformational practices that will change your organisation for the better. Ultimately, these books aren't really describing management, or HRM, or work; they are doing the twenty-first century equivalent of peddling snake oil – miracle cures for all organisational ills. The problem with these Happy HRM books is that they don't really get us anywhere. The 'evidence' they offer is enthusiasm, anecdote and assertion. And the practices they advocate are backed up by evangelical rhetoric rather than reasoned argument. More worryingly, there is no room for debate. OK, so that's a very academic point of view but when academic studies are well designed they can tell us whether a practice works, and why, what its limitations are, where it is completely ineffective and (occasionally) what can be done about all this. Happy HRM, by contrast, is a take-it-or-leave-it approach. It'll work because we're all fired up to do it, all enthusiasts, all believers, all cheerleaders. If and when it doesn't there's no real explanation (other than the organisational equivalent of your faith not being strong enough). Good studies provide building blocks which help us understand more about people and organisations, just as studying medicine provides evidence about the human body. Happy HRM is simply a question of faith. If it works it's magic. If it doesn't you're lost with no guide to the path.

The aim of this book, by contrast, is to explore and explain the truth of what happens at work. It is not being written to market a new HR practice, nor popularise a consultancy firm, nor will it make you feel inspired, enthused or overjoyed (though obviously it will be nice if you are). I hope that this approach means that, if you ever do become a manager, you will be a better, more thoughtful and more well-informed one. It should certainly enable you to understand the realities of the workplace.

This chapter sets the scene by considering what HRM is. It is also the theory chapter. And for everyone who flinched at the word theory – Don't Panic. It isn't difficult, it doesn't take long and it should more than repay any attention you give it because while practices tend to change (and in HRM they tend to change all the time) theories, if they are any good, are pretty resilient. So while knowing about something like managing diversity or empowerment or performance related pay will keep you going for however long the fad lasts before being re-named, re-structured and re-vised, knowing a few of the theories behind the HR practices will enable you to assess any others that come along, to understand why problems arise and to chuck a few phrases into essays that are guaranteed to impress your tutors. So if you're going to skip anything (and transform a very short book into a really amazingly titchy one) then keep the theory and skip something else.

What is HRM?

So what is HRM anyway? Is it something special, a particular (and particularly sophisticated) set of practices that are linked to strategy or is it just the personnel department going through a bit of re-branding and changing the sign on the door? If it is something different, a qualitatively distinct approach to managing people, then a certain number of features are key. Storey's (1995: 5) definition is that:

Human resource management is a distinctive approach to employment management which seeks to achieve competitive advantage through the strategic deployment of a highly committed and capable workforce, using an integrated array of cultural, structural and personnel techniques.

He also provides a table of key beliefs and assumptions, strategic qualities, the critical role of managers and key levers (1995: 6) (see Table 1.1).

Table 1.1   The HRM model

---

1.   *Beliefs and assumptions*

- That it is the human resource which gives competitive edge
- That the aim should not be mere compliance with rules, but employee commitment
- That therefore employees should be very carefully selected and developed

2.   *Strategic qualities*

- Because of the above factors, HR decisions are of strategic importance
- Top management involvement is necessary
- HR policies should be integrated into the business strategy – stemming from it and even contributing to it

3.   *Critical role of managers*

- Because HR practice is critical to the core activities of the business, it is too important to be left to personnel specialists alone
- Line managers need to be closely involved both as deliverers and drivers of the HR policies
- Much greater attention is paid to the management of managers themselves

4.   *Key levers*

- Managing culture is more important than managing procedures and systems
- Integrated action on selection, communication, training, reward and development
- Restructuring and job redesign to allow developed responsibility and empowerment

---

Source: Storey, J. 1995. 'Human resource management: still marching on or marching out?' In *Human Resource Management: A Critical Text*, edited by J. Storey. London and New York: Routledge. p.6. Reproduced by permission of Cengage Learning EMEA Ltd.

This is a distinctive approach to managing and being managed that aligns both human and strategic aspects of work. Way back in the mists of time (well, actually the 1980s and 1990s) this was an important, or at least a much rehearsed, debate. Gone were the days of demarcation, fixed job grades and negotiations with trade unions and welcome to the Brave New World of the 'can do' outlook with highly committed workers going beyond contract to please customers, harmonised terms and conditions, learning organisations and individual contracts. This was a whole new relationship between workers and management centring upon harmony and trust.

Of course it didn't really happen like that. In some (mainly very large) companies there were changes in the way people were managed, elegantly documented by researchers like John Storey (1992) which were called HRM. But there were also plenty of firms which had taken the HR approach for many years (including John Lewis, and Marks and Spencer) but which labelled it personnel management and even more which changed the label but not the practices. So empirically the distinction between HRM and non-HRM was never clear cut, yet despite this HRM was hailed as both new and different. Part of the reason for that is that innovation is always interesting and continuities tend to attract far less publicity than change. I don't think any newspaper or academic journal is ever going to boast a headline along the lines of 'Shock News: Employment Practices stay the Same'. Novelty is attractive and novelty sells so we exaggerate the extent to which things change. Far too many academics (and even more journalists) assume that history starts the moment they set foot in a firm, that whatever they are told is new, is new and that anything that happens after that moment is entirely attributable to whatever it was that was new. It's a pretty naïve approach. But talk to anyone who has been working for about 20 years in the same place (amazingly this is still the average job tenure in Britain) and they will more than likely tell you that it has all happened before – different label but the same idea. Pay very close attention and they might even tell you what happened.

Frankly, it is not particularly clear whether the first academics to write about HRM (Beer et al., 1984) were putting it forward as an idea to think about or a prescriptive model for the way managers might approach the people they employed. Whichever it was, HRM soon became known as a theory of work, a model for managing and a description of practice; terminology which had a significant impact but which was not necessarily particularly accurate (Noon, 1992). By the start of the 1990s, some writers on HRM were claiming credit for the demise of personnel management (which hadn't happened), massive workplace change (which had happened in some places, but only some and even there might not have been so very different to changes which had gone before) and the decline of union membership (a genuine and dramatic social change which had little to do with HRM. In some US companies, employers did take a 'bouquets and brickbats' approach to discouraging unions, often beating up activists while providing nice HR practices for employees so they felt no need to organise, but it is not clear how widespread this was, and in Britain unionised organisations were *more* likely to have HR practices).

Needless to say there was a huge discussion about this and researchers delighted in pointing out the incongruities in the debate. Most of the elements of practice and approach that HRM valued had also been valued by personnel management and the only reason the two areas did not look identical was that empirical descriptions of personnel management were compared to aspirational prescriptions for HRM; workplace realities contrasted with ideal and idealised situations (hardly a fair basis for comparison). To complicate matters still further, if HRM was a particular thing or group of things, no-one could agree on exactly what those things were: A link to strategy? Managing culture? Empowering workers? Harmonising terms and conditions? Getting rid of trade unions or welcoming them in as partners?

Anyway, it wasn't a particularly interesting debate and it went on for years. I apologise for bothering you with it but it does help to explain the approach I'm taking to HRM in this book because I am not doing any of that. I promise that at no stage will I break off and ask you whether HRM really is different from personnel management or ask you to describe the differences. Because if I did we would have difficulty getting beyond the limitations imposed. Definitions of HRM vary. Whichever one we chose, assuming that we decided that HRM was indeed a distinctive approach to the management of people, we would find that in practice only a tiny minority of firms would conform to all or part of this definition (not all of which would call their practices HRM). Pretty well all of these firms would be large organisations. What we might then do is hope that our readers forgot just how selective our evidence had been and assumed that any conclusions applied to all firms. Alternatively, there is the option that many of the HRM books (including this one) espouse, which is to accept the fact that HRM has become the popular label for anything about work. The authors then write about work as a whole and just label it HRM.

The way I will be using the term HRM is as a synonym for anything to do with work and employment. Or, as Boxall and Purcell (2011: 1) put it:

HRM refers to all those activities associated with the management of work and people in organisations.

Realistically, this is the way it is used in practice in quite a few textbooks and business schools. For many business students, the HRM course is the only module they have on anything to do with work and it would be unfortunate, to say the least, if it made no attempt to engage with the realities of the workplace beyond a favoured few firms and workers. Of course, HRM is not a particularly good synonym for work. The name suggests that people are resources, only worthwhile for the contribution they make to work, and that our focus should be on management (or managing, or managers). There is even a book, titled *Human Resources* about vampires who 'take over' their target organisation and its employees in a very literal way. Personally, I have always refused to have the term HRM in my academic title and (unless and until my employers read this, realise what's going on and try to insist) I am Professor of Work and Skills. It's neutral, it doesn't make it sound as though I am only interested in managers and (other than people actually working in the area) no-one has the foggiest idea what it means. All to the good. However HRM is the title we've got so let's make the best of it.

Unitarism, pluralism and radicalism

Unitarism, pluralism and radicalism are all different frames of reference; ways of looking at the workplace and interpreting what happens (Fox, 1966). Put simply, *unitarism* is the assumption that management and workers share the same outlook (and that outlook is usually defined by management); *pluralism* argues that each will have different viewpoints, that such differences are natural, and that managing these differences is what the employment relationship is all about; while *radicalism* asserts that differences between employers and employees are natural, inevitable and permanent, and they can and should never be reconciled (Edwards, 1995).

One of the main distinguishing features between good and bad studies of HRM, to my mind at least, is the perspective they take on workers and the workplace. At its worst, HRM does have a tendency to be *unitarist*. In other words, writers assume that there is only one perspective on work and that is management's. Workers exist to carry out management's directions (with varying degrees of efficiency) and everybody shares the same goal. The workplace is a team with managers as coaches, urging workers on to greater efforts. So managers can, do and should speak for the whole organisation; they share its interests and their perspective is the only one that is relevant, legitimate or even (in some texts) exists. Mike Noon and Paul Blyton (1997: 1) started the first edition of their book, *The Realities of Work* with the words:

> Here is a modern myth about work. Contemporary workplaces are peopled by high performing, highly committed individuals, bound together into a common cause by a corporate mission enshrined within a strong organisational culture. Workplaces themselves have been 'transformed' by new technologies, new forms of organisation and a new generation of management thinking that stresses flexibility, quality, teamwork and empowerment. The workers in these establishments are motivated by ambition and a sense of purpose, and by the individually-designed financial rewards they receive – part of those rewards taking the form of a financial stake in their organisation, either as shares or as profit-related bonuses. Employees are guided by self-interested individualism, and no longer see a role for collective organisation and representation, hence the demise of trade unions.

Sounds lovely and encompasses almost every element of HRM. When it is put like that, you know it's a myth and I know it's a myth, but it's amazing how many books are written on the assumption not only that this is true, but that it describes the vast majority of workplaces.

The key aspect of unitarism is the assumption that only management matters. It is a perspective that allows no room for other views, different interpretations or alternative understandings of the workplace. All conflict is pathologised, since the only reason anyone can have for disagreement is that they are troublemakers, or mentally ill, or both (it is this view that pitches union reps as 'managers of discontent'). But differences of opinion are a normal and natural part of working life. After all, workplaces may be filled with harmony, inspiration and personal fulfilment through achievement (as the celebratory literature claims) but they are also the sites of bullying, harassment, low wages, dull jobs and a whole range of pressures from managers, suppliers, customers and clients. Globally, more people are killed at work than in war (Taylor, 2009). While each year in Britain 30,000 women are sacked for being pregnant, and this despite the fact that legislation exists to protect them (Hinsliff, 2009). Less dramatically, staff may be told to work long hours of overtime but not claim payment, since this would be 'disloyal' to the firm (Grugulis and Vincent, 2009); cleaners may be low paid (Dutton et al., 2008: 119); and, in some firms, managers regularly scream at their subordinates to encourage them to greater efforts (Hochschild, 1983). Under these circumstances surely dissent is natural and the question we should be asking is not how to make these workers more productive, but how to make work less exploitative.

Even in the happiest and best managed workplaces people are going to disagree with something. Some years ago a couple of academic colleagues (Tony Dundon, Adrian Wilkinson) and I did research into a small consultancy company. The professionals there were well paid (two pay rises a year), had plenty of fringe benefits, did interesting work, were trusted and most were pretty happy with their work (something also attributable to the fact that the company went to a great deal of effort to recruit a certain 'type' of person, including interviewing candidates while dressed as Mickey Mouse, but that's another story, see Grugulis et al., 2000). As part of this project we did a short survey of employees which included satisfaction questions and something like over 90 per cent of respondents replied that they were happy there and would recommend the company to a friend. We were amazed. You almost never see satisfaction ratings that high. Then we went into the boardroom to present and the company were amazed too. Where were these dissatisfied workers? What were their names? How dare they tell us (outsiders) of their problems without going over them internally first? Could we hand over the results identifying each individual respondent? Well yes, we could, but we didn't. It was a pretty revealing incident. A well-managed company, where people genuinely enjoyed working but which had zero tolerance for those who were not totally satisfied.

Conflict is natural in the workplace. A theory that cannot accommodate this and that looks only at one group of workers (the managers) is not a particularly good theory because it doesn't explain the realities of workplace life. A far better perspective on work is *pluralism*. Pluralism sees the workplace as a miniature democracy, rather than a unitary team; there are common interests but there are also diverse ones and conflict, disagreement and varying perceptions of the same activity are a natural consequence of this. Think of the phrase 'A fair day's work for a fair day's pay', which has long been a trade union slogan. No-one would disagree with it as it is an entirely reasonable statement, yet in practice managers and workers often spectacularly fail to agree on exactly what levels of work or pay constitute 'reasonable'. That's pluralism.

This means that a key task at work is to manage the differences that exist. So organisations may want to give workers a voice in the workplace, to air their grievances, represent their interests and ensure that communications flow smoothly. Works councils can provide a forum for employees to be consulted on issues and trade unions can help to represent their interests. These structures will not make the differences disappear, employers and employees will not be reconciled; but they can work together and consultative structures can help to manage that process.

Radicalism is different. It sees the divisions between employers and employees as permanent and enduring. The very nature of the employment relationship is that workers are exploited. That exploitation may be hidden or overt, but it always exists, so it is in workers' interests to resist management wherever and whenever possible.

Each of these approaches – unitarism, pluralism and radicalism – are frames of reference, or points of view, or ways of looking at the world. They are important and it is important for us to understand them since the way we view work and what happens at work depends heavily on what assumptions we make about each of the various stakeholders. A unitarist might assume that a strike had been caused by individual troublemakers; a pluralist that it demonstrated a failure to manage the natural differences between employers and employees; a radical that it was a sign that workers were developing their ability to express their own interests. All very different viewpoints, which are likely to result in varying ways of tackling the issues from identifying and disciplining the discontents, to sitting around a table and talking, to helping with class consciousness. So appreciating not only our own frame of reference, but also those of others, is important.

Let's make it even more complicated. The interests of employees and employers can differ, but they don't always. In other words, there is a partial coincidence of interest (beautiful phrase) between employer and employee. And work cannot be totally predicted in advance. You might think it can, after all most employees have employment contracts, but, unlike almost every other legal contract, employment contracts are incomplete. They specify some duties but always have a catch-all phrase covering anything else their employer might want them to do. (I've just checked mine. Its catch-all is 'and will be required to undertake such academic and administrative duties as may reasonably be allocated to them from time to time'. And phrases like 'reasonably' or 'from time to time' leave rather a lot of room for interpretation.)

In practice then, work is a negotiated order. Employers don't pay for guarantees that a job will be completed, they purchase the *capacity* to do work. Employees don't necessarily know exactly what they will be doing from their employment contract; their job is worked out (negotiated) over time. Such negotiations are rarely formal. Rather, tasks and responsibilities are given, assumed or withheld; the intensity and pace of work and the speed of production are praised, criticised or not mentioned; and this effort is exchanged for pay, prospects or promotions.

These negotiations, implicit and explicit, formal and informal, are not conducted on a level playing field, since the power relations at work are unequal. Sainsbury's has a great deal more negotiating power than Mrs Bloggs of 47 Acacia Avenue. When Mrs Bloggs signs a contract with

Sainsbury's (that Sainsbury's have written) then contractually she is not only agreeing to their terms and conditions, their pay rates, their job design, their holiday arrangements and their working hours, she is also agreeing to being given orders. If Sainsbury's fails to fill a post then it is an inconvenience; the other stockists or cashiers or managers or directors will have to work that extra bit harder. If Mrs Bloggs fails to get a job it is a disaster: she won't be able to feed the kids or pay the mortgage and if she is unemployed for a long time it's probably goodbye to 47 Acacia Avenue.

So, work involves structural differences built in to unequal power relations with working practices often implicitly negotiated and plenty of room for mistaken assumptions on both sides. This is much more interesting than the Happy HRM books, though admittedly, the stories are not likely to end in quite the same way.

Rhetorics and realities

Given these differences, divergences, structural antagonisms and varying assumptions about work it should come as no surprise to learn that one of the most common accusations against HRM is that its promises don't actually match its practice, to the extent that Karen Legge (1995) subtitled her best-selling book on HRM *Rhetorics and Realities*. This is, as Sisson (1994) notes, an optimistic model that aims for economic efficiency as well as improving the quality of working life, but its rhetoric often camouflages an unpleasant reality.

There are a number of reasons for this dissonance. The first is HRM's much vaunted 'business focus' which means that while its justifications are all couched in terms of developmental 'soft' HRM; its realities are cost-cutting 'hard' HRM. TSB managed to announce a new culture change programme to increase trust, at the same time as sacking a few thousand staff, who first learned their fate from a report in the *Financial Times* (Blyton and Turnbull, 1992). The second is that, gauged on the basis of the grandiose claims they make for themselves, many HR practices simply *cannot* work. According to *The Independent* newspaper, some years ago Chicony Electronics had as its mission statement:

> Our ultimate goal lies not only in the pursuit of perfection and excellence, but also the creation of [the] well being of all [of the] human race.

This was slightly ungrammatical, beautifully ambitious and almost certainly unachievable. The news story suggested that aiming for perfection and excellence probably diverted attention from the Thai women workers it employed in its Scottish factory who were paid slave wages, deprived of their passports and bussed between the factory and segregated residential blocks to keep them away from the other workers (*The Independent*, September 1999).

Table 1.2   The 'HRM organisation' – rhetoric and reality from Sisson (1994:15)

Rhetoric	Reality
Customer first	Market forces supreme
Total quality management	Doing more with less
Lean production	Mean production
Flexibility	Management 'can do' what it wants
Core and periphery	Reducing the organisations' commitments
Devolution/delayering	Reducing the number of middle managers
Down-sizing/right-sizing	Redundancy
New working patterns	Part-time instead of full-time jobs
Empowerment	Making someone else take the risk and the responsibility
Training and development	Manipulation
Employability	No employment security
Recognizing contribution of the individual	Undermining the trade union and collective bargaining
Team-working	Reducing the individual's discretion

Source: Personnel Management: A Comprehensive Guide to Theory and Practice by Bach, Stephen and Sisson, Keith. Reproduced with permission of Blackwell in the format 'Book' via Copyright Clearance Center.

The third is simple cock-up. Contrary to the assumptions in the celebratory literature most organisations, whatever they do and whatever sector they are in, are not hives of flawless efficiency. Poorly thought out plans, duplicated work, inconsistent orders and contradictory messages are part of the realities of work as Weeks' account of culture change in a British retail bank makes clear:

Each day, each manager will receive a pile of circulars with descriptions of new initiatives, and, less frequently, obituaries of old initiatives. Confusion does not result just from the cacophony of contemporaneous culture initiatives introduced Bank-wide (ranging during the period of my fieldwork from Progressing the Vision to Organisational Culture Inventory to Performance Culture Inventory to Learning Culture Strategic Review to UK Branch Banking Core Values Programme) as well as more locally (a number of regions were doing their own culture and values work, as were Head Office departments such as Network Strategy and Development, with its Service Improvement Programme Values and Behaviours initiative). It results also from the plethora of other initiatives, programmes, projects, pilots and directives that overlap with or contradict the culture-change efforts....

Consider, first, two of these initiatives, both associated with the Bank's Vision: the Organisational Culture Inventory and the Performance Culture Inventory. As the interchangeability of their names suggests, the two programmes were strikingly similar. They were both run by Head Office departments – the 'Corporate Quality and Change Management' Department in one case and the 'High Performance Managerial Competencies (HMPC) Unit' of the 'Personnel and Consultancy Services' Department on the other. I found it remarkable that the obscurity of these and other department names was not more often a target of derogation in the Bank. Both programmes were running at the same time. Both had the aim of changing the culture of the bank to create the attitudes and behaviours required to achieve the Vision of becoming First Choice. Both programmes involved the use of outside consultants, and both assumed the possibility of quantifying culture and the necessity of measuring it against a pre-determined ideal. The Vision being rather vague, however, it was not obvious what the ideal attitudes and behaviours required to achieve it were. The two programmes settled on different ideals. (Weeks, 2004: 112–113; reproduced with the kind permission of University of Chicago Press)

Two different departments with two different versions of bank culture both running in parallel. Unsurprisingly, presented with errors of ignorance, weakness and deliberate fault, staff are not slow to pick up on the differences between what they are promised and what they experience and they judge their employers accordingly. When The Gap devised a new mission statement of Words to Live By and distributed copies to every employee the employees responded with their own version (see Table 1.3).

Workers are neither mindless believers nor cultural dupes. They may genuinely appreciate and engage with an HRM initiative but they may also reject, resist, be cynical about, mock, or simply ignore it and quite a few of those reactions can be predicted by looking at the employment context outside the individual HR practices to consider what employees do, what they are paid, how they are treated and what else management

Table 1.3 The Gap, Words to Live By

The Gap **The Gap** **Words to live by**	**The Gap** **Words to live by** *Staff Contributions in Italics*
Everyone counts	Everyone counts *the days until they leave*
Every difference makes a difference	Every difference makes a difference *apart from indifference*
Own it, do it, done it	Own it, do it, done it *EH?*
Less is more … simplify	*Our wages* Less is more … simplify
Take the smart risk	Take the smart risk *and quit*
Do it better every day	Do it better every day *and still feel shit*
Do the right thing	Do the right thing *and leave*

Source: Grugulis and Wilkinson (2002)

does to them. Grand promises made against a background of neglected grand promises are unlikely to be believed.

This is particularly important since the language of HRM is often phrased in 'motherhood and apple pie' terms, using words which have positive connotations and with which it is impossible to disagree. So, for example, pay (a fairly neutral term) and compensation (which has implications of money given in exchange for the worker undergoing unpleasant experiences) become reward, which is extremely positive. Involvement and team-working are both positive phrases and who would wish to substitute rigidity for flexibility? But when we look at the practices in detail 'reward' may conceal low wages, 'involvement' poor communication and 'flexibility' employers distancing themselves from oppressive supervision and unsafe working practices.

One of the best, and funniest, responses to all this management-speak is Scott Adam's character, Dilbert. Dilbert is a US-cartoon office worker, and he and his colleagues (put-upon Alice, hopeless Wally and Asok, the permanent trainee) face numerous office perils which include their ill-informed pointy haired boss and Catbert, once Dilbert's cat but now the evil, clever and manipulative HR director (says it all doesn't it?). Adams claimed that he got the inspiration for these cartoons after spending eight years in a cubicle (for non-office dwelling life forms a cubicle is a partition in an open-plan office, about chest height, that completely fails to fulfil any of the functions that old-fashioned walls used to do). In one of my favourites the pointy haired boss announces in a meeting that, 'I used to say people are our greatest asset but I was wrong. We had a survey and cash is our greatest asset. People came eighth'. 'I hate to ask what was seventh' murmurs Wally to Dilbert. 'Carbon paper' replies the pointy haired boss. The website is at http://www.dilbert.com/ I recommend it – it is much more entertaining than doing work.

Once you have enjoyed the Dilbert website feel free to come back to the book. It covers some of the key HR topics and discussions, offers evidence from real workplaces and robust studies and tries to make sense of both the advantages and the disadvantages of various initiatives. It starts, in Chapter 2, by examining HRM and strategy as well as the links between HRM and organisational performance. Interestingly enough there are some, but these do not take the form that most HR managers would want you to believe. Chapter 3 deals with skills and training, one of the most popular HR practices and also one of the most misunderstood. It examines the ways that skills are limited by or developed through work and considers the prospects for a Knowledge Society. Chapter 4 presents pay in a whole host of different forms, from generous executive pay to time and performance based systems, to minimum and living wages. In Chapter 5 we explore flexibility and the nature of contingent contracts for those at the bottom of the labour market as well as the privileged professionals at the top. Chapter 6 considers employee voice, both as participation – the form advocated by pluralists in which employees have a say in workplace practices – and involvement – the management-initiated and task-focused form of voice which is now far more common. Chapter 7 considers the service sector, the area where most of the workforce are located, the nature of 'high touch' service jobs and the idea of the emotional proletariat. Finally, Chapter 8 considers briefly what work might look like in the future, both optimistically and pessimistically, and whether employers are betraying their part of the bargain. In such a short text we cannot hope to provide comprehensive coverage of every HR topic, but we hope that you find this selection informative, interesting and revealing.

Discussion and conclusion

Let's get rid of one last hangover from the Happy HRM crowd before we go on to think about what happens in practice: the idea that somehow HRM exists to make workers happy. I'm not entirely sure how this belief arose. It's certainly a hangover from personnel times but as a view of either HR practices or the specialist HR function it is not particularly helpful and it could simply distort understanding. To be clear, the HR function is not there to represent employees to management or to act as some kind of neutral third party when problems arise between employees and management. They are management. They are employed by the firm to do a number of administrative functions (payroll, record keeping), they sometimes have a hand in recruitment, they may design or advise on HR practices and processes but they aren't neutral. Nor is it particularly useful to think about producing happy workers because no-one is aiming for that. The HR department may introduce some initiatives that may be helpful – dignity at work, fairness, equity, respect and even being sensible (though heaven knows that is in short supply in most places) – but this is not neutrality and the HR department is very firmly on management's side.

Interestingly enough, writers of fiction have never made the mistake that these Happy HRM writers do, and assume that all work is fulfilling, rewarding and interesting. Charles Dickens offers grim accounts of work in Victorian England. Robert Tressell's (1914/1957) *Ragged Trousered Philanthropists* not only provides details of the daily experiences of workers but also shows how these philanthropists subsidised the better off. Orwell and Huxley both show vividly how incredibly dull, routine and tightly controlled work can be. And Stuart MacBride's unfortunate Detective Sergeant Logan Macrae has to put up with quarrelling and unreasonable bosses, long working hours and lack of sleep as well as his own mistakes. Of course work can be interesting, engaging, fulfilling and enjoyable. But it can also be dull, routine, demeaning and difficult. If fiction writers do not forget that then neither should we (although here, I promise, the examples will be grounded in fact).

Is HRM Strategic?

When the term HRM was first coined a key distinction that the early writers drew between HRM and old-style personnel management was that HRM was strategic and personnel management was not (Storey, 1992; Walton and Lawrence, 1985). This was a slightly unfair distinction, since old-style personnel managers had also hoped for a seat on the board and emphasised their contribution to the business as a whole, so the wish to link employment practices to strategy was not new. A rather more reasonable question might be, not whether HRM wants to contribute to business strategy, but whether it actually does, and that is what this chapter considers.

It deals with the various debates and dilemmas around HRM and strategy. It starts with a brief review of what strategy is, before going on to draw out the nature of HRM, distinguishing between HRM as 'best practice' (one coherent and integrated 'bundle' of mutually reinforcing practices) and HRM as 'best fit' (practices designed to fit the organisation). It also discusses the link between HRM and performance, which is far more complicated than most of the enthusiastic assertions of HR managers would have us believe and questions whether what we are reviewing is simply the search for a 'good employer' with HRM as a rather unreliable proxy.

What is strategy?

A strategy is, quite simply, a plan for the future. Most businesses will have a plan. It may or may not be written down. It may or may not be detailed, but the plan exists. Classical writers on strategy would not have counted anything as strategic unless it was formal, written and generally initiated by top management. This is what might be described as the idea of strategy as the 'general in his tent'. The general sees the external forces (or armies) which impact on the firm – the competitors, the nature of the product markets, the economic situation – and issues orders accordingly. The Chief Executive at the top develops the strategy and the people below put it into practice. Porter (1980, 1985) views strategy as market positioning and focuses on the way that firms compete in order to differentiate themselves from their competitors. So, a firm might compete on the basis of low prices, the quality or distinctiveness of their goods and services, or take up a particular market niche.

While classical strategists look outside the firm for their inspiration, the Resource Based View (RBV) looks inside. It focuses on the internal resources, such as brands, or expertise, or experience, through which firms can compete and which, because they are 'inimitable' and 'non-substitutable', should give companies an advantage over their competitors (Boxall and Purcell, 2016).

More recently, accounts of strategy have sought to capture the extent to which it is an iterative process. Mintzberg (1987) likened strategy to craft, drawing the analogy of a potter at the wheel. The potter knows what shape the final piece of pottery should be and works towards that, but they also respond to variations in the clay, adjust the speed of the wheel and add water as they work. Whittington (1996) observed the way that strategists actually operate, and focused on the *process* of developing strategy. Strategists work on both daily practice and future direction, combining the nitty-gritty detail of mundane work with plans for the future and using each to inform the other. Following these approaches strategy is not pre-planned by the people at the top but, rather, emerges from action.

Each of these are very different approaches with varying implications for the way firms are managed (Whittington, 2000) as well as for HRM. In the classical approach to strategy, which relies on careful and thorough planning, and in which plans are cascaded down from the top, HR practitioners are downstream of the planners. Their role is to implement those plans. This may be by ensuring that the right numbers of people are present, with the right skills, when and where the plans indicate they are needed. Of course, the problem with such a simplistic view is that it seldom matches reality. Many organisations simply do not have a clear, written strategy and, when they do, it is not often widely disseminated. In one study, while 84 per cent of head office managers claimed their company had an overall philosophy on people management, few could articulate it and almost none of their responses matched the HR practices actually reported in their organisations. As Marginson and his colleagues (1988: 116–120) somewhat politely concluded, in practice, firms' approach to strategy was 'pragmatic' and 'opportunist' rather than planned.

What then of the RBV? This is very popular among HR writers since, in it, internal resources are central to competitiveness so HRM is a key contributor to organisational performance, and it certainly makes sense for firms to compete on the basis of their unique competencies, as well as to check that they have the necessary 'table stakes' to engage in a particular market. However, as Kaufman (2015) points out, most writers on the RBV fail to follow their own arguments through to their logical conclusions. The literature is replete with examples of HR practices that had positive outcomes for businesses, but few of these are, in the words of the RBV, inimitable or non-substitutable. Given this, successful practices are very likely to be taken up by other firms, effectively limiting or neutralising their advantage. Barney (1991) cites the example of Continental Airlines, which had the worst on-time record for its flights, until management established an incentive programme, offering employees $65 every month that the airline came first. Continental rapidly shifted from last place in the league tables to first. So far so good, but, as Kaufman points out, this is a fairly simple scheme that is very easy to imitate. If this were all that were required to top the on-time tables then surely Continental's competitors would also have introduced similar schemes. When HR practices are generic, it is difficult to fit them to the RBV logic. There is a stronger argument that individual people can be the inimitable and non-substitutable assets which enable a firm to compete but not all employees are uniquely and distinctively valuable resources (Boxall and Purcell, 2016), and distinguishing between valuable and 'worthless' employees could well be invidious.

Of these views it is Whittington's (1996), on strategy as practice, that most accurately captures what developing strategy is like. In this process strategy is reciprocal; it not only influences HR practices but is itself influenced by those practices. This is a key insight since it appreciates the shared nature of strategy development. Under this approach HR responds to business strategy but strategy also responds to HR. The disadvantage of this approach is, because of its fluidity, it is hardest to pin down in studies. As Legge (1995) points out, HRM can really only be matched to business strategy if we adopt the rational, classical approach. It is much harder to trace a link through an evolutionary strategy (although the links in such an approach are likely to be no less strong).

'Best practice' versus 'best fit'

Just as the term strategy can incorporate a range of different practices, so too can HRM. One key question which writers on HRM are concerned with, is whether there is one best way to implement HRM ('best practice') or whether HR policies and practices should be tailored to the needs of each individual firm ('best fit'). This has been a fairly contentious debate.

'Best practice'

The idea behind best practice is that there is one superior bundle of HR practices which result in positive outcomes regardless of the nature of the business, the labour market or the product or service being delivered. This idea goes under a number of acronyms: High Performance Work Systems (HPWS), High Commitment Work Systems (HCWS), High Commitment Management (HCM), High Involvement Management (HIM) and High Performance Practices (HPP), but the underlying assumptions of each are essentially the same. Jeffrey Pfeffer (1998: 75) puts forward seven key 'best' practices that all firms should aim to deploy:

1. Employment security
2. Selective hiring
3. Self-managed teams or team-working
4. High pay contingent on company performance
5. Extensive training
6. Reduction of status differences
7. Sharing information

There is good sense in linking these together and it is fairly easy to see how such practices reinforce one another. High pay may attract more applicants, enabling firms to hire selectively. Once recruited, extensive training will help these talented people to build their skills, so that they are better able to contribute to organisational objectives, while team-working will provide a vehicle for that contribution. Reducing status differences will facilitate the team-working process and sharing information can assist this contribution as well as celebrating triumphs. Finally, having recruited such high calibre staff, trained them extensively and involved them in workplace decision making, it also makes sense to provide them with employment security.

This is an attractive bundle and Pfeffer is genuinely attempting to create a 'high road' approach to managing people. However, it does need to be treated with caution. Not all of these practices are as 'best' as they seem, nor is it clear who they are actually 'best' for. Generous executive pay may be good for the individual executive, but it is less likely to benefit a company's shareholders or its other employees (Legge, 1995). Many HR practices conceal work intensification (Marchington and Grugulis, 2000). Even employment security may not be as 'best' as it first appears. Pfeffer quotes the example of Lincoln Electric, where employment security could be offered because 70 per cent of employees' pay came from profit sharing. This made it much easier for the firm to provide security in straitened circumstances, but at the cost of employees' pay declining dramatically. Welcome as employment security is, there must surely be a point at which it is simply not economically viable for employees to continue working.

Then too, as the jumble of acronyms at the start of this section reveals, while best practice writers agree that there is one bundle of best HR practices, there is no consensus on what that bundle should consist of. Pfeffer's seven practices are listed above (in his earlier writings he proposed 16), Huselid (1995) suggests 13, Delaney et al. (1989) identify 10, while Wood (1999) opts for a generous 17. Different models with varying practices all put forward as the one best way of doing HRM.

Even when different studies commend the same practices they may interpret them differently (Marchington and Grugulis, 2000). So selective hiring can be the 'number of applicants per position' (Delaney and Huselid, 1996), the 'proportion administered an employment test prior to hiring' (Huselid, 1995) or the use of psychometric and other sophisticated selection tests (Patterson et al., 1997). Similarly, training can mean the extent to which training is disseminated through the organisation (Huselid, 1995), the inclusion of broad training not relevant to the immediate work task (Arthur, 1994), that training is safeguarded in budgets (Wood and Albanese, 1995) or that it results in 'increased promotability within the organisation' (Delery and Doty, 1996). All useful, all commendable, all different measures. The lists are also culturally specific. As Boxall and Macky (2014) point out, Huselid, conducting research in the USA, considers the use of a formal grievance procedure evidence of best practice. In the UK and elsewhere this is actually a legal requirement.

Most seriously, these lists are all sanitised and exclude many of the genuine strategic decisions that businesses have taken over the last few decades, including downsizing, delayering, outsourcing, the growing use of flexible and contingent labour, joint ventures, supply chain partners, divestments and acquisitions (Purcell, 2001). It is difficult to argue that the best practice lists can retain credibility when they omit real HR decisions as practised in many organisations.

The best practice writers focus on the impact that HR practices have on organisational performance (for more of which, see below) and it is fairly easy to see that for the convenience of anyone trying to link HR to performance it certainly helps the research if HRM is one consistent and coherent set of practices. In reality of course it is not, and only a small minority of firms deploy the sort of HR bundles that the best practice writers describe (6 per cent, according to Charlwood, 2015).

To summarise, there is no consensus on how many practices constitute the 'best' practice bundle, nor what these are, nor how they should be implemented. It is not clear who the practices are best for and the real, and often unpleasant, decisions actually taken by HR departments are carefully excluded from all of these lists. Perhaps most fundamentally, as Purcell (1999) and Boxall and Purcell (2016) point out, HRM cannot be both 'best' practice and strategic. If there is one 'best' way of doing things that should apply regardless of context then we cannot argue that HRM is an integral and bespoke part of a business' strategy.

'Best fit'

This is where the idea of 'best fit' comes in, which is that HR practices should be tailored to each organisation. Beer and colleagues (1984) suggested three different models of firm: bureaucratic, market and clan. Each has different characteristics and requires its own particular approach to managing people (Boxall and Purcell, 2016). *Bureaucratic* organisations operate in fairly stable environments and are often large. The civil service, large retail banks and the NHS might be classified as bureaucratic. According to the model, these organisations are primarily concerned with control and efficiency so their HR systems may be characterised by authority, hierarchies, job descriptions and job evaluation. *Market* oriented firms, by contrast, are located in more fast-paced environments, such as advertising or high fashion. They treat their employees like subcontractors with relations characterised by short-term exchanges and rewards for performance. *Clan* firms seek long-term adaptability from their staff. Here workers are bound together by diffuse kinship links, shared values, team-working and a strong commitment to the firm.

Other authors suggest tailoring HRM to different aspects of the firm, such as its size, the stage it is at in the lifecycle, whether it manufactures one product or many, or the skill levels each process requires. Boxall (2003) differentiates between low-skill workers providing mass services in cost-based markets, highly skilled workers competing in markets that are differentiated on the basis of quality and expertise, and firms where there are a range of skills and a mix of cost- and quality-based competition (see also Arthur, 1994; Sorge and Streeck, 1988).

This contingent approach, while equally sanitised from references to downsizing, delayering and outsourcing, does allow HRM to be strategic, in the sense that practices can be tailored to the individual business. But there is no one element of an organisation which absolutely determines strategy and from which HR practices can be simply read off, which means that, useful and logical as the contingency models are, they do not always match practice. Organisations can and do take different approaches to the same market challenges, they may adopt employment practices which vary considerably from those that the models suggest 'should' be implemented, and they are likely to need to juggle a whole host of tensions, which impede the implementation of neat, coherent policies.

So British Oxygen and Air Products, both bottled gas suppliers faced with the same industry challenges, met them in different ways: British Oxygen by upskilling their drivers to deal with customer service, Air Products by outsourcing and deskilling deliveries (Boxall and Purcell, 2016). Sophisticated HR practices can be found in managing low-skilled call centre work (Kinnie et al., 2000), and low-skilled care assistants responded more positively to these practices than their more highly skilled nursing colleagues, reporting higher levels of autonomy, affective commitment and job satisfaction as well as lower levels of turnover intention (Harley et al., 2007).

The textbooks may suggest that competing on the basis of low-margin, high-turnover ('pile it high and sell it cheap') is linked to low-wage, low-skill work, while high-margin, niche competition is linked to more highly skilled work; and for most firms this is indeed the case. However, Aldi, which certainly piles goods high (often still in the boxes they were delivered in) and sells them cheap, offers shop-floor employees a starting rate of £8.40 rising to £10 per hour (its competitors offer close to the National Minimum Wage rate, £6.70 an hour for over 21s at the time of writing this chapter in spring 2016). Workers are expected to be highly skilled and to work intensively. The quality is good, products are cheap, service is rapid and there is definitely no help with packing. Its sales are rising and it has won the *Which?* magazine Supermarket of the Year award four times in the last seven years.

While Aldi combines low-margin, high-turnover work with high skills and high pay, Lloyd's (2005) research into the fitness industry demonstrates that even when staff are a key aspect of the service being sold, 'premium' products are not necessarily linked to premium skills in staff. Fitness instructors were predominantly young and low paid (as little as £5–£6 an hour at the time of her research). Even premium membership-only gyms looked primarily for personality in recruitment, seeking people who were (2005: 23): 'easy going, bubbly, very friendly, customer friendly' or 'sociable, gregarious, fun'. And while some recruiters insisted on degree-level qualifications several confirmed that (2005: 25): 'We look for nothing in terms of qualifications … communication is the key' and 'We start with anybody … some have no relevant qualification'.

The clear message is that this is not deterministic. Rubery and her colleagues' (2004) account of a multi-client call centre provides a vivid demonstration of the tensions inherent in the company's HR systems. The call centre did try to harmonise its contracts and to use the prospect of permanent contracts as an incentive for staff, but their attempts to match employment policies to the nature of the work were constantly disrupted by clients, to the extent that the client with the lowest skill requirements and lowest work intensity offered the highest rates of permanent contracts, because this was what the client wanted.

In other words, nice as it is to have models which link specific HR practices to firm characteristics, or strategies, or skill levels, and logical as these connections often are, real organisations are rarely that simple. Many do match the carefully thought out models but social systems are complex and, in real organisations there is no set 'list' of HR practices that can be read off from the product or labour market context to be applied to the firm. Managers may have their own ideas about ways of competing. Firms may mimic each other, adopting practices because their collaborators and competitors use them, because they are popularised by consultants and professional HR staff or simply because they are fashionable. This is probably an argument for contingent HR systems, but implemented in ways that are much more complicated, confused, and incoherent than the literature suggests.

HRM and performance

The principal assumption underlying much of the HRM literature, including that on both best fit and best practice, is that good HRM contributes to organisational performance. Intuitively this makes sense. Workers who are well-trained and possess the appropriate skills, who are given a voice in how work is done and rewarded for the input they make to company performance should (surely) work better and contribute more than those who do not have the skills to do their jobs, whose voice is ignored and whose effort is not rewarded. However, much as we would like to believe that good HRM inevitably and inexorably results in improved performance, and despite a lot of assertions from HR managers (and others) that it does, the evidence is not at all straightforward, nor does it all point in the same direction.

There are three issues that we need to address before we can confidently assert that HRM improves performance. The first two are practical: it is difficult to agree on what either performance or HRM actually are. Performance can be assessed by a whole host of different (and often complicated and contradictory) measures. And there is no one single definition of HRM. The third issue is theoretical since, even when HR practices are correlated to good performance, there is nothing to indicate that they *cause* that performance (Grugulis and Stoyanova, 2011). Let us consider each of these in more detail.

The first issue is that there is no one, single accepted definition of performance. Remember this if you are ever asked to write an essay about anything 'and performance'. Normally I discourage students from starting essays with a definition. When terms are not contested it can take up valuable space, distract them from making points which would earn marks and simply result in a lot of very tedious essays. That said, there are some occasions when it is wise to be clear about what you mean, or at least show that you know that the term can mean different things, and this is almost always the case with performance. In the private sector performance can be assessed financially but even here there are multiple measures. It can mean profit, or share price, or market share, or dividend yield, or dividend cover. And a firm may report positive results for only some of these by, for example, choosing to cut costs (and so reduce its profits) in order to secure greater market share or limiting dividend payments so that it has funds to invest in the business. On top of these fairly straightforward measures, accountants also assess performance against a whole host of different ratios: return on capital employed; profit before interest and tax; current ratio; gearing; cash flow and many others. These results will be affected by a number of factors, not all of which are connected to HR including currency movements, or the decision to take over another company. To further complicate matters, some aspects of company accounts are matters of choice, with activities undertaken and revenue attributed to particular areas to take advantage of allowances or minimise liabilities. Financial performance is not straightforward and the financial performance of the organisation as a whole is not simply the financial performance of the shop-floor writ large.

Nor are monetary measures the only gauges of performance. Most organisations are assessed on many different performance metrics. In the public sector we encourage hospitals, schools and police authorities to balance their books every year, but few would commend their performance if, to achieve this, a hospital killed half their patients, or a primary school failed to teach its pupils to read, or a police authority decided to stop all front-line policing. Less dramatically, all of these organisations will be audited by their own professional bodies, and their internal performance metrics are likely to require them to do well on the measures used by the inspection teams. In the private sector too, performance may be judged on the basis of service levels, quality products, well-managed distribution systems or volumes handled.

Not only are there a range of (often contradictory) performance metrics, but we also need to decide whose benefit we are assessing. Are we demanding a positive return for shareholders, or senior managers, or employees, or the government? Given that our interest is in HR policies and practices we might want to consider performance measures around employee well-being such as commitment, satisfaction, turnover or absenteeism. After all, if HR practices do impact on performance then presumably this is because they affect employees in some (positive) ways, so it makes sense to measure these. Batt (2002) suggests that the key areas which impact performance are that employees should have the abilities, motivation and opportunities to participate (or, as she calls it, AMO). Clearly, performance is a whole range of different things, assessed by varying metrics, at diverse levels.

Our second issue, as we have already seen, is that HRM can mean a range of (very different) practices. There is little consensus about which practices constitute the HRM bundle, or even whether there should be a bundle in the first place. Some practices are popular in most of the definitions of best practice HRM, and Boselie and his colleagues (2005: 73) rate the top four HR practices as training and development, contingent pay and reward, performance management and careful recruitment and selection. But not even these appear in all lists and some practices that are clearly important, like employment security, appear in very few (Marchington and Grugulis, 2000). Even when appropriate bundles are put into practice, we do not know which practices are particularly important and which are marginal.

The third issue, once we have accepted definitions of both HRM and performance, as well as a series of suitable performance measures that are themselves measureable, is to establish whether the results observed have been *caused by* HRM. This is important. Many studies have established that there is a *link* between profits and more and better HR practices, but it may be that firms which perform strongly and make good profits have the additional resources to spend on good HRM, rather than that HRM *causes* good performance. In other words, we have a problem of *causality*.

Let us examine the evidence for this. Back in the 1980s and 1990s there were a number of large-scale surveys which asserted firmly that HR practices were clearly linked with firm performance. Huselid (1995) found that greater use of HRM was positively associated with lower turnover, better productivity and higher profits, regardless of which strategy the firm adopted (see also Delery and Doty, 1996; Patterson et al., 1997).

So far so good. However, as later researchers were quick to point out, these studies suffered from a number of flaws. Many relied on single respondents, who were likely to know their own specialist area of the firm well, but who might not be as reliable a source when asked about other departments. Practice and outcomes were assessed at a single point in time. This is much easier for the researcher, who does not have to return to their research site or rely on respondents completing a survey a second time, but it raises questions about the research (Boselie et al., 2005; Boxall and Purcell, 2016). After all, even if HR practices do result in positive outcomes, there is likely to be a time lag between introducing the practice and reaping the benefits. If increasing and improving training (for example) results in higher quality products, lower levels of wastage and improved health and safety then this can best be assessed by examining practices both *before* and *after* the new training practices are introduced. The danger of studies conducted at only one point in time is that these show *correlation* (that two things can be observed together) rather than *causality* (that one has resulted in the other). This is a common feature of statistical studies and novice statisticians are frequently entertained by spurious and comic correlations. In the USA, for example, the divorce rate in Maine mirrors the consumption of margarine; mozzarella seems to be slightly more academic in its effects, since per capita consumption is correlated to the number of civil engineering doctorates awarded; while the rise and fall in revenue generated by ski-ing facilities matches that of deaths caused by people becoming entangled in their bed sheets. But while no-one suggests that mozzarella consumption helps engineering doctorates (though we could devise a nice theory about the pizza eating proclivities of engineers), many do confidently assert that HRM boosts performance. The truth is, that from the data we have, we simply do not know this.

Some studies have tried to address the methodological limitations of the early research. David Guest and his colleagues (2003) conducted a longitudinal study, assessing both practices and performance over a number of years. They found that HR practices were linked to lower labour turnover and higher profits per employee, but productivity was not higher, and crucially, when past performance was taken into account the results ceased to be significant. In other words, the best predictor of good performance in the present was good performance in the past. The association between HRM and performance was confirmed but there was nothing to show that it was the HRM which had resulted in the good performance.

This area is tangled since, unlike the models used by statisticians, we cannot hold various factors stable while we investigate individual variables. In real life factors will impact on each other, so employees are likely to be more satisfied when market conditions are good and organisations perform strongly. When investigated in more detail, the data we have suggests that, while there is a link between HRM and good performance, it is not that HRM results in good performance, but that good performance results in HRM, perhaps because profitable firms have more resources to invest in their employees.

HRM and the 'good' employer

It is entirely possible that what is being captured in many of these studies is not the efficacy of HRM, but whether or not an employer is a 'good' employer (Guest, 2011). This is a significant point. If the positive association between HRM and performance simply captures decent treatment, then the specific HR practices deployed, are, if not irrelevant, at least less significant. It may not matter, for example, whether firms have the latest consultation mechanism or the most fashionable means of delivering contingent pay. Rather, as seen in Chapter 1, what may matter is the fact that practices send messages to employees (Purcell, 1979). So, what counts is that there are positive investments in employees, that employees have a voice in the workplace and also that there is an absence of negative behaviours such as bullying, discrimination and arbitrary treatment.

This also brings us to an important caveat. If what we are seeking are 'good' employers then HR practices are a pretty unreliable proxy. Decent treatment does not always take the form of sophisticated HRM, and sophisticated HRM does not necessarily mean decent treatment. Nick Bacon's (1999) research into a steel mini-mill noted an impressive array of HR practices including extensive training and management development with 88 per cent of the workforce holding a vocational qualification, multi-skilling and team-working, all supported by good salaries, the use of contingent pay, generous fringe benefits and individual performance appraisals. However, in tandem with these, there were also some less attractive practices. The trade union was derecognised and workers still believed to be members were put under 'surveillance' out of working hours. While the company paid full fees for all workplace training, courses were always scheduled outside working time and were not voluntary. The Personnel Director said, 'we will terminate the contract of anyone who refuses training' (1999: 8). Absenteeism was reduced to one per cent, because anyone absent more than five times in a five year period was disciplined, and workers off sick were put under pressure to return to work or take the time as holiday. According to three of the employees (1999: 11):

> I was 'persuaded' to take holidays for these three days off sick on the grounds that if I did not everybody would lose part of their [bonus] payment that month.

> [I went home after an accident] every day the medical centre phoned asking when I would be coming to work. For the last two days the Personnel Department also phoned. The last day [a manager] told me that if I didn't come to work the next day at my next assessment I

would be penalised ... I fell at work again and was pressurised into returning to work early.

During sick leave I have received phone calls asking me to change my sickness or accidents into paid holiday leave, this is a common practice, in which you are not asked but told to take holidays to save accident reports.

When the company's safety award was suspended, because of questions about its health and safety reporting, workers were called in to the manager's office one by one and required to sign a petition to ask for it to be reinstated. As Bacon points out, in any survey this company would tick all of the sophisticated HRM boxes, but it is difficult to argue that this was a 'good' employer.

Even when firms do not directly intimidate their employees, the mere presence of an HR policy or practice is no guarantee that it will be implemented, nor that it will be implemented effectively. Woodrow and Guest (2014) report on a hospital with an exemplary anti-bullying policy where levels of bullying actually rose to way above the national average because this exemplary policy was simply not put into practice. The policy itself was incredibly time consuming and managers were discouraged from implementing it by their superiors. According to one (2014: 9):

It's almost as though there are two sets of rules: there is the policy, and then there is different people's interpretation of that policy ... senior people would be telling me: 'you can do this, but don't do that. Do the next bit, and maybe just let that go for a little while.' Then you start to think: 'if I let it go, am I protected? Do my senior managers think that I'm doing a bad job because I'm sticking to policy?'

In other words, the presence of sophisticated HRM and the development of impressive (and even exemplary) policies do not necessarily translate into good management on the frontline.

Discussion and conclusions

So how far does this chapter get with helping with the question of whether HRM is strategic? Some key points are worth pulling out. The first is that HRM cannot be one 'thing', one group of practices, applied consistently across all contexts and also be strategic. As Purcell (2001) points out, this is not an issue that we have to face in other areas of management. Marketing is not one bundle of practices, applied regardless of context, nor is operations management. We also need to be cautious about some of the implications that commentators draw from such best practices, namely that organisations can be trusted to take the HR 'high road', obviating the need for trade union or state intervention (Purcell, 1999). Nothing in the evidence we have seen from firms suggests that management can always be trusted to act in workers' best interests, nor that the interests of management and workers invariably coincide.

The drive to make HRM coherent seems more likely to be based on researchers' desire to draw out its links to performance than on any empirical or theoretical reasoning. That said, one valuable point can be drawn from the best practice discussion, and that is the way that HR practices can be mutually reinforcing. It does make sense to implement HRM in integrated 'bundles' although we probably need a lot more evidence on what practices should constitute each bundle, which are central and which are peripheral, as well as how and why (and possibly whether) these bundles work in practice.

Of course, from the point of view of whether HRM is strategic or not this does not matter since anything can be strategic as long as the employment practices *fit* the corporate strategy. In other words, if a company's strategy is to minimise costs and its employment practices involved paying wages at below the level of the minimum wage, eliminating most HR initiatives, refusing to recognise trade unions and stripping employees of benefits then those practices could reasonably be considered to be strategic. Not nice, but strategic because they fit with the strategy.

With the best fit discussion, it certainly makes more sense to fit HR practices to each individual firm and there are models in the literature which provide guidance on this. But real firms are complicated arenas with varying imperatives, tensions and conflicts. And real firms also involve managerial (and client, and supplier) choice. All of these elements can and do influence the HR practices that firms deploy. All of these elements are changeable and many clash.

Mix these in to the modern understandings of strategy as iterative, processual and reciprocal and it is really not easy to tell which actions are strategic and which are not. Links to strategy are certainly much easier to read if we adopt the classical understanding and seek out careful plans passed down the hierarchy for action. So is HRM strategic? In some firms yes, but with the proviso that that strategy, as well as the HR practices and policies devised to enact it, is subject to change.

What of HRM and performance? This is also an important debate, not least because it is generally conducted so badly with assertions substituted for evidence. Of course we would all like to believe that good HR practices result in performance improvements but, as Guest (1997) so cogently points out, to do this we need a theory of HRM, a theory of performance and a theory of why the two are linked. As this chapter has shown, we do not yet have any of these. HRM, even in studies that confidently assert it is one coherent bundle, can mean a wide range of practices, performance can be gauged by a whole host of measures, privileging various different stakeholders, at a number of levels of analysis and the reasons for improvements in performance are barely touched on in existing studies. We do know that HR practices are linked to good performance, but the majority of our evidence suggests that this is because profits result in HRM, rather than HRM results in profits. We also need to be cautious, given the differences of interest that exist in the employment relationship, where good performance for one party is bought at the expense of the others.

It is also possible, and indeed quite probable, that in this debate HRM has become a proxy for the 'good employer'. To a certain extent this is legitimate. For a good employer one would hope to see an absence of bullying, inconsistent treatment, harassment and so on. But positive treatment can be expressed in a whole range of different ways and, as our evidence has shown, the existence of good HR practices is no guarantor of a good employer. To address this we need to go beyond lists of practices and consider how initiatives are put into effect (Boxall and Macky, 2014; Guest, 2011).

Where does this take us? Possibly to the point that HRM, like most aspects of social systems, is much too interesting to be simple. There are no lists from which employers can read off practices to be linked to strategies, nor are there straightforward rewards for implementing set practices. Rather, our evidence shows a mixture of good and bad employers, confused and coherent implementation and strategic and tactical approaches.

Skill in the person is the aspect of skill we are most familiar with. It encompasses educational and vocational qualifications, expertise, the experience a worker may have gained over many years on the job, and soft or social skills. An expert surgeon, informed by a range of tests and using touch and sight, knows how deep to make an incision; a mechanic will listen to an engine running; a chef will smell fresh vegetables to confirm their quality.

Skill in the job is different. It covers the demands and limitations of work, the tasks allocated, the way work is controlled, the discretion that is allowed or withheld. Jobs can *constrain* skill as much as they can enable it. In the 1936 film *Modern Times* the hapless Charlie Chaplin starts out working on the conveyor belt in a factory tightening bolts on a panel; he tightens, the belt moves on, he tightens, the belt moves on. The next two workers hammer the bolts in place, each repeating one short action over and over again as the belt moves. This work is dehumanising. Chaplin has no control over what he does, nor the pace at which he does it since it is the factory manager who speeds up the pace of the line, and even when Chaplin leaves his workstation to go to the toilet (for a sneaky cigarette) he is unable to stop twitching and jerking in time to the bolt-tightening actions. His job is so totally deskilled that, whatever his abilities or talents, he can contribute nothing to it. Such work is commonplace today. McDonald's provide staff with a 600-page 'Bible' that prescribes every action within each restaurant. Buns arrived pre-sliced, ketchup dispensers squirt a precisely measured amount of ketchup and buzzers and lights time production and ensure that no discretion is exercised (Royle, 2000). Call centres can script staff's encounters with customers (Taylor and Bain, 1999). In all of these jobs staff are required to follow rules and routines, tasks are regimented and individual discretion firmly curtailed.

The same job can be designed in very different ways. Felstead and his colleagues (2007) distinguished between fitness instructors who worked on pre-packed routines and those who choreographed their own. The pre-packaged material were widely recognised brand names which dictated the outfits the instructors wore, the routines they taught, the scripts they delivered and even the jokes they made. Updated and new routines were issued several times a year and compulsory instructor training sessions ensured that everyone was up to speed with them. By contrast, the freestyle instructors simply drew up their own routines, selecting music and moves that they thought would work well together.

Clearly these are dramatic examples and most jobs involve a mixture of constraints and freedoms. So supermarket head offices set out a shop's stock, prices, display planograms, hours of work and staff's terms and conditions of employment but it is local managers who allocate detailed working rosters and deal with customers (Grugulis et al., 2011).

Equally, jobs can be designed to *develop* skills. Asaf Darr's research investigates the work of IT specialists who design bespoke computer systems (2002, 2004). These professionals often spend many weeks based in clients' premises and working with their computer staff to design a system that fits clients' individual requirements. Since each system is bespoke and the design work is a co-operative process, developers require high levels of both soft and technical skills.

In other words, jobs vary, from routinised work on the factory line and cooking French fries in McDonald's to the development and design of complicated computer systems; work can limit skill as much as it can develop and sustain it.

The third way of describing skills is *skill in the social setting*. Skills are, after all, social entities, socially enacted and constructed so it is hardly surprising that the social judgements of workers impinge on assessments of those skills. So we assume that high status people do high-skilled jobs. Steiger (1993) describes the hierarchy of skill on a construction site. There skilled workers were the high status ones and their tool-boxes were of both practical use and a key symbol of this status. However, by the time of his research, plumbers' materials had changed so instead of having to work with difficult lead pipes they fixed pre-formed plastic ones which demanded far less skill. Despite this, and despite the fact they no longer needed tools, these plumbers kept their skilled status, boasting that (1993: 539): 'anybody can do it with the proper tools. A good mechanic can get by without the proper tools'. Other workplaces are similarly slow to adjust hierarchies when skills change and skilled workers seem adept at adjusting to reorganisations assuming team leader roles and preserving their place in the hierarchy (Bacon and Blyton, 2003).

Just as skilled workers may preserve their status when work changes, so factors from outside the workplace may be imported and affect evaluations of skill. This is famously true of gender and time and again researchers have shown that jobs are judged differently by both employers and the workers themselves, depending on the skill of the person doing the job, with women's skills consistently degraded and men's enhanced. This inflation of the skills involved in men's work and deflation of those involved in women's work was so common that Green and Ashton (1992) commented in exasperation that there was no longer any point asking an employer whether a job was skilled or not because the only thing the researchers learned was the *gender* of the person doing the job. As with gender, so with race and class and social hierarchies; prejudices which exist outside the workplace which denigrate women, BMEs and the working classes also operate within the workplace to devalue their jobs, regardless of content.

This is not to argue that skills are entirely socially constructed, products of a worker's position on the status ladder. Skills involve real work and an individual's expertise, as well as the freedom they are allowed in the workplace, can make a difference. But it is a timely reminder that workplaces are not technical havens which exist away from the social maelstrom of the outside world. Sexism, racism and a whole host of other bigotries are real and really are experienced in the workplace. One result of this is that social judgements about individuals are also likely to affect judgements of their skills.

Human Capital Theory

One of the best known theories about the way education and training impact on skill, and particularly skill in the person, is Becker's (1964) Human Capital Theory (HCT). Becker argues that, just as investing in plant or machinery can result in greater rewards (a higher rate of return) so, with people, investing in educational qualifications and skills will also result in a higher rate of return. Workers with higher qualifications are likely to earn more, are less likely to be unemployed and, when unemployed, are much less likely to be unemployed long term than those with no or few qualifications.

Human Capital Theory is an insightful idea and, to a certain extent, it works. In the UK only 48 per cent of people with no qualifications were working, compared to over 80 per cent of people with at least one qualification (ONS, 2014). Workers who have graduated from college earn more than those who have only completed high school, and those who have completed university earn more than one with only a college education (Green, 2006). So far, so successful. However, Human Capital Theory does not work all the time and, even when it does, it is by no means the whole story. There has been a great deal of research into pay gaps and, while some can be explained in Becker's terms (higher levels of qualification, women's caring responsibilities and maternity leaves), a considerable pay gap still remains between men and women and whites and BMEs (see Chapter 4 for a discussion of the gender pay gap). The unfortunate truth is that workers are paid different levels of pay for a whole range of reasons, including sexism and racism. Moreover, while there are clear pay premia for particular qualifications, not all qualifications are fortunate enough to attract additional payments since payments are made, not for skill, but for market value. Fluency in German, Latvian, Chinese and Sanskrit are all skills, but each is likely to attract very different rewards for reasons unrelated to their complexity. And of course not all qualifications are of high quality. Indeed there are some vocational qualifications that are so weak they do not attract any pay premium at all (Grugulis, 2003).

In other words, while Human Capital Theory holds true for some qualifications and some people it is not a complete explanation of the way the labour market functions nor why different people are paid varying amounts.

Learning at work

All this reinforces earlier warnings about viewing HR practices in isolation. Training courses might be easy to count but they do not really tell us much about how and what people learn at work. For that we need to know about what they do, how challenging it is, how much autonomy and discretion they have and over what. Some of my favourite questions from the extremely well-designed *UK Skills Survey* are those that ask how long respondents took to learn to do their job and (very telling this) how long it took to learn to do it *well*. Fifteen years in to being a full professor and I feel as though I'm just beginning to touch on what I need to know (I suspect I will still feel this way in another fifteen years, such is the nature of the job).

This means that, if we are interested in how to develop staff and how to do it well the answer is not simply training but attending to a whole host of wider variables in the workplace. Lave and Wenger (1991) captured this beautifully in their study of the way work groups learn. They argued that novices started as peripheral participants, they could carry midwives' bags, watch butchers cut meat or fetch the tea and coffee in a self-help meeting. As time went on and they learned more about the work, they took on increasing numbers of tasks, rising over time to full members of the group.

This is a revealing insight. After all, learning is not a separate, independent and reifiable phase confined to the start of a profession or a particular training course; it is part of social practice. Alison Fuller and Lorna Unwin (2004) drew on Lave and Wenger to develop their *expansive* and *restrictive* approaches to learning (see Box 3.1). *Expansive* workplaces encourage learning. Workers have access to a number of different groups ('communities of practice') both within and outside their organisation so that they can tap into the collective memory and acquire external knowledge, skills are valued and development is encouraged, expertise is defined broadly and workers have access to knowledge-based qualifications. By contrast, in *restrictive* workplaces, tasks are narrowly defined and training, where it exists, focuses workers on narrow job roles, there is little boundary-crossing in work nor access to outside groups. Learning is on-the-job and is expected to be over and done with as quickly as possible with staff expected to move rapidly to 'full participation'.

Box 3.1   Expansive and restrictive approaches to learning

← Approaches to Workforce Development →	
EXPANSIVE	RESTRICTIVE
Participation in multiple communities of practice inside and outside the workplace	Restricted participation in multiple communities of practice
Primary community of practice has shared 'participative memory'; cultural inheritance of workforce development	Primary community of practice has little or no 'participative memory'; no or little tradition of apprenticeship
Breadth: access to learning fostered by cross-company experience	Narrow: access to learning restricted in terms of tasks/ knowledge/location
Access to range of qualifications including knowledge-based VQ	Little or no access to qualifications
Planned time off-the-job including for knowledge-based courses and for reflection	Virtually all-on-job; limited opportunities for reflection
Gradual transition to full, rounded participation	Fast – transition as quick as possible
Vision of workplace learning: progression for career	Vision of workplace learning: static for the job
Organisational recognition of, and support for employees as learners	Lack of organisational recognition of and support for employees as learners
Workforce development is used as a vehicle for aligning the goals of developing the individual and organisational capability	Workforce development is used to tailor individual capability to organisational need
Workforce development fosters opportunities to extend identity through boundary crossing	Workforce development limits opportunities to extend identity: little boundary crossing experienced

Reification of 'workplace curriculum' highly developed (e.g. through documents, symbols, language, tools) and accessible to apprentices	Limited reification of 'workplace curriculum'; patchy access to reificatory aspects of practice
Widely distributed skills	Polarised distribution of skills
Technical skills valued	Technical skills taken for granted
Knowledge and skills of whole workforce developed and valued	Knowledge and skills of key workers/groups developed and valued
Team work valued	Rigid specialist roles
Cross-boundary communication encouraged	Bounded communication
Managers as facilitators of workforce and individual development	Managers as controllers of workforce and individual development
Chances to learn new skills/jobs	Barriers to learning new skills/jobs
Innovation important	Innovation not important
Multidimensional view of expertise	Uni-dimensional top-down view of expertise

Source: Fuller, A. and Unwin, L. 'Expansive learning environments: integrating organisational and personal development.' in Workplace Learning in Context, edited by H. Rainbird, A. Fuller, and A. Munro. London and New York: Routledge. p.130 © 2004. Reproduced with permission of Taylor & Francis Books UK.

To illustrate this Fuller and Unwin (2004) describe a manufacturer of bathroom showers which employed about 700 people and which had a long-established apprenticeship programme with many ex-apprentices rising to senior management. Apprentices gained experience of different departments through structured job rotations, studied knowledge-based qualifications at college and attended residential courses to improve team-working. Contrast this with a small company of about 40 employees which provided steel polishing services. Apprentices here were confined to one department (steel polishing), were expected to be fully competent in a narrow range of tasks after one year and were enrolled only on a low-level competence-based qualification (NVQ) for which they learned on the job. As the expansive–restrictive continuum so clearly illustrates, in order to understand the way people learn at work, as well as to appreciate the strengths and limitations of that learning, we need to think about the job they are doing, the levels of discretion they can exercise, the workplace they are in, the work groups and communities of practice they have access to, the way they are managed, their opportunities for progression, innovation and discretion as well as the training they have access to. Put simply, skill is about not only the person, but their job and the context that job is located in.

Formal training

As Fuller and Unwin's (2004) distinction between expansive and restrictive workplaces reminds us, training and development itself can take a whole range of different forms, which vary in their value, and particularly in the value that they have for the employee. Training which is restrictive may well benefit employers, since it enables employees to perform a narrow range of tasks better or to be more efficient at their job, but it is likely to have few advantages for employees since it will neither make their current work more intrinsically satisfying nor prepare them for other, more complex and better paid, jobs. In their call centre research Callaghan and Thompson (2002) observed one call centre representative referred to remedial training when his tone was insufficiently enthusiastic. Such a workshop would be likely to ensure that his employer's (aural) corporate image was consistent, with representatives' voices rising and falling at the right moments, but would have few advantages for the individual call centre worker. In work, interactions with customers were guided by scripts and conformity was monitored.

At the other end of the spectrum, professional qualification-based training not only provides workers with new skills, which may be used for the benefit of their employer, it also certifies those skills and adds considerably to lifetime earnings. For the major 'big four' accountancy practices, accountancy is a graduate entry profession and for the first three years graduates are required to take professional examinations. They attend residential courses, study for knowledge-based exams and work on different client projects with tasks and responsibilities becoming more challenging over that time period. Once they are qualified they are required to undertake regular continuing professional development to keep their knowledge current.

During the 1990s the volume of training in the UK rose to a peak of 15 per cent of the workforce in 2003, but after this it fell to 13 per cent and between 2006 and 2012 training volumes fell by about a third. This fall was particularly marked in long courses, off-the-job training and training for women. Employers report that they are 'training smarter', doing more at a lower cost by focusing on shorter courses, more on-the-job learning and online modules. Clearly, given the problem of low-quality jobs and low-quality training such a change in emphasis must raise questions about training quality. These questions are hard to answer. There is a great deal of detailed qualitative research into vocational training which explores the quality and rigour of workers' learning but such investigations are necessarily focused on a small number of organisations while few surveys attempt to capture training quality. The 2012 *UK Skills Survey* (Green et al., 2013) is one exception, and it included questions on the nature of training to try to explore whether quality was also falling. These included whether the training was certified; whether it improved the informants' skills; whether it made them think about different ways of doing their job, helped them improve the way they worked or helped them enjoy their job more; and whether the training needed to be memorised. Using these indicators it seemed that, just as training itself was unequally distributed so, to a far greater extent, was high-quality training with workers who were already highly qualified receiving twice as much long training as their less well-qualified colleagues and much more likely to report that training makes them think while the less well qualified are more likely to experience training where work needs to be learned off by heart (Green et al., 2013).

So, just as jobs vary, so too does training in terms of skill, quality and rigour. Instead of being a means of equalising opportunity in the workplace it is a way of further differentiating between those with varying levels of skill and education. Training is like a hospital for the healthy with the people who already have had most education benefitting most from it.

Comparative systems

There are a whole range of different ways of approaching vocational education and training (VET) and different countries tackle this in very different ways. It is worth briefly looking at some of these differences, if only to stop us believing that the practices we are most familiar with are natural, inevitable or the only system possible.

The three key factors here are capital, labour and the state, as well as the relationship between them (Ashton, 2004). Nations may be voluntarist (market based), in that they choose to leave the market to its own devices. In voluntarist nations the role of the state is to encourage the free functioning of the market. They may also be regulated (co-ordinated), and in co-ordinated market economies the role of the state is to intervene to prevent market failure (when firms avoid training their workers because they fear that trained workers will leave for jobs elsewhere).

Each of these systems can work well, but in different ways, and each has their own weaknesses (Grugulis, 2016) as these four examples illustrate. So, in the USA, a liberal market economy, in Silicon Valley, California cutting edge skills are supported and developed by informal learning as well as formal courses. Here the proximity of world-class universities provides a steady stream of talented new recruits, while active alumni networks facilitate skills development and problem solving by linking expert workers socially. The existence of an industry cluster makes job mobility easier since workers can switch employers without having to move house and without their children changing schools, and this mobile pool of expert workers also help to pass best practice round different firms.

In Singapore there is a market system, but the state also invests directly in training and development, building and extensively subsidising high-quality vocational education and training including through the At-Sunrice Global Chef Academy. In 2011 the government funded a new building with dedicated Western and Asian kitchens, state of the art cook–chill facilities and dedicated space for a Wine Academy and Coffee and Tea Academy. Intensive tuition in the academy is combined with placements in Singapore's top restaurants. Expert faculty and high-quality facilities enable the college to offer high-quality training to students, and to attract students from all over the world.

In Germany, where VET is co-ordinated by employers' associations, trade unions, educationalists and the state the majority of young people enrol on high quality apprenticeships on leaving school. These qualifications combine classroom study with on-the-job learning with tasks and projects designed to demand and develop apprentices' skills. Apprentice wages are low, but fully qualified professionals boost their career potential by completing an apprenticeship.

In China the economy as a whole is state controlled, but there is a growing private sector. VET is erratic. State-owned enterprises provide most and there is some excellent provision in privately owned firms with levies to support training. But, while vocational colleges have good guidance about linking class- and work-based study, those in prosperous areas are significantly better resourced and equipped and some qualifications can be disrupted by college agreements with local factories to provide all students to work on assembly lines. So while some placements are valuable opportunities to learn skills (Jürgens and Krzywdzinski, 2015), others, such as those at Foxconn, put students of Chinese herbal medicine, secretarial services, hotel and tourism, English, horticulture and accounting on the assembly line (Smith and Chan, 2015).

Each system has its own strengths and its own corresponding weaknesses. In the USA cutting edge, high level skills can be found in a number of areas, but the levels of intermediate skills are low because there is no system pushing people towards vocational qualifications, nor any agreed standards for such qualification. In Germany, where the support systems ensure that the majority of the workforce are qualified at intermediate level in the area they work in, high level skills are comparatively neglected.

The differences between market and co-ordinated countries are clearer in theory than they are in practice. Even in the UK (an unregulated, market economy), education is provided free to all to the age of 18 and numerous government subsidies are devised to encourage organisations to train more (often with the unfortunate result that firms simply chase subsidies, changing their training systems to suit). Moreover each VET system is supported by market and labour market conditions: sectoral pay bargaining in Germany means that workers gain little financially by moving employers; light touch bankruptcy legislation in the USA permits failed firms to write off their debts and entrepreneurs to try again.

Knowledge work

There are a whole host of different ways to learn, to acquire and develop skills and to demonstrate them in the workplace, in suitably knowledge-intensive jobs. And it is this search for knowledge work which (often implicitly) underlies much of HRM. Indeed, one of the main drivers behind the advocacy of best practice HPWS was the hope that, by changing the way people worked, HRM could stimulate knowledge-based competition (Boxall and Macky, 2014). This is the reason that skills and training have always attracted interest from national governments with administrations from all parts of the political spectrum focusing on them, investing in them and hoping to structure their economies around them.

The idea of the Knowledge Economy, a nation where work is dominated by highly skilled knowledge work, and which competes primarily on the skills and knowledge of its citizens is an attractive one and there is some evidence to back it up: people are becoming more highly educated, many jobs do demand more skills and, in some sectors, routine jobs have been automated. As Reich (1991) pointed out, between the 1950s and the 1990s the proportion of knowledge workers (or 'symbolic analysts', who work with ideas, concepts and symbols rather than physical goods) rose from 8 per cent to 20 per cent of all workers. In the Knowledge Economy most routine work would be automated or outsourced, often to other countries, emphasis would be put on schools and higher education with increasing numbers attending universities and work would be highly skilled and knowledge based.

Knowledge jobs certainly exist. Many of these are traditional occupations which have always been highly skilled, such as lawyers, architects and doctors; others are more recently developed jobs including advertising executives and consultants; yet others are products of technological innovation, such as software designers and systems analysts. This is work in which the skills of the workers are key, and are often constantly being developed. Individual workers possess a great deal of technical know-how, much of which is tacit and an extensive literature has developed on the distinctive (and generally collaborative) ways such knowledge workers can and should be managed.

Often this involves high levels of discretion. Starbuck (1993) describes the way Wachtell Lipton, an exceptional New York law firm, operated. They would hire the most brilliant and outstanding scholars from the best universities and give them the most challenging and specialist legal cases to work on. Every lawyer in the firm had an open door policy and colleagues were encouraged to discuss and consult each other. A small kitchen contained supplies of cookies, soda, coffee, cakes and fruit so lawyers could arrive in colleagues' offices with edible gifts from the kitchen, then consult on problems. Here staff developed by working on challenging problems and being able to draw on others' expertise.

The management practices in these knowledge intensive companies are often pleasurable to read about because their aim is to keep the workers socially engaged and co-operative, so effort is put into good management. Professionals may be given flexibility in their schedules and places of work, while supervision may be limited and light touch with 'carrots' favoured over 'sticks'. In his research on a major pharmaceutical company McKinlay (2000) describes the way teleconferences would be enlivened by project co-ordinators encouraging US participants to open birthday cards or boxes of European biscuits online. Such practices are intended to encourage collaboration and knowledge exchange. Nonaka and Takeuchi's (1995) book, *The Knowledge Creating Company* details the way that engineers and bakers collaborated to produce a bread-making machine.

Less frequently featured in the literature (perhaps because companies generally grant research access during the good times) are the occasionally painful and often amusing examples of organisations that get it wrong when managing knowledge workers, often when trying to codify the elusive tacit knowledge. Medical sales agents, on being told that they would be rated on the number of contacts they made in any given month promptly started to include everyone they met on their databases (nurses, doctors, accountants) whether or not these people were relevant to securing sales (Hayes and Walsham, 2000). Staff whose knowledge gives them power, influence or security are unlikely to co-operate with managerial attempts to strip them of that knowledge. One bank, attempting to rationalise its more than 150 separate internal intranets into one shared system, found that staff were setting up electronic fences to protect their own territories (Newell et al., 2000).

As this text has pointed out, there is only a partial coincidence of interest between employees and employers. The good HR practices described by Starbuck, McKinlay, Nonaka and Takeuchi are positive ones and designed to foster collaboration but there is another side to Knowledge Management and that is the codification of knowledge. Indeed Hansen and colleagues (1999) distinguish between knowledge management *personalisation* strategies which encourage knowledge sharing between people and *codification* strategies which seek to record what is known within the business and encourage its re-use.

Both strategies can be successful. Dow Chemical's knowledge management programme catalogued their (highly disorganised) data archive and, as a result, the company now earns a significant income from licensing its technologies (Scarbrough and Swan, 2001). But this codification is rarely associated with knowledge work, discretion or light touch management practices; rather it controls interactions between staff as well as between staff and customers.

This means that we need to approach the literature on knowledge management with care. It certainly encompasses highly skilled occupations, reviewing ways to make them more productive, more sociable and to foster the exchange and development of knowledge; but it also catalogues, codifies and sets out acceptable practices, providing managers with more tools with which to monitor. Particular caution is needed since the term knowledge work is a complimentary one that managers may actively seek, whether or not the jobs so labelled involve knowledge.

A wise student of HRM will dutifully note when work is called knowledge work but will also look at what each occupation involves and decide for themselves whether the label is deserved. Some commentators claim that all service sector work is knowledge work, a claim that is difficult to defend. Clearly service sector work encompasses many very highly skilled jobs including accountants, lawyers, doctors, teachers and university professors but it also, and in much greater numbers, covers security guards, care workers, call centre representatives, cleaners and barristas – jobs in which it is harder to identify high levels of knowledge, expertise and discretion.

This is an important distinction since, at one stage, it was fashionable for social commentators and management gurus to predict the rise of the knowledge economy in which almost all jobs would be interesting, highly rewarded knowledge work with mundane, poorly paid tasks automated out of existence. A prediction that clearly has not been realised. Knowledge work exists and some knowledge occupations are managed in ways that make the rest of us envious, but these are, and probably always will be, only a small elite when compared to all the jobs in the economy. In the UK Skills Survey, the number of low- and un-skilled jobs still outnumbers the number of intermediate and highly skilled ones (Green et al., 2013).

Conclusions

So where has this chapter taken us with skills, training and development? It has introduced Cockburn's (1983) tripartite definition of skill: skill in the person, skill in the job and skill in the social setting. This is valuable since it helps us to identify the various factors hindering or enabling skills development. It also focuses attention firmly on the systemic aspects of skill. Jobs matter, and highly skilled workers trapped in jobs where they cannot exercise those skills are likely to become frustrated and alienated.

People can learn in formal and informal ways, developing by working on challenging tasks with expert co-workers, as well as on set training courses. And training courses can be restrictive and non-developmental just as much as they can help to foster skills. We have also looked at different international systems, where support is provided or withheld and where organisations provide or limit skills-based training. Some of the results of our observations were encouraging. Every system has its strengths and encourages development in particular ways. Others were less so, with much formal training, and much of the high quality formal training restricted to workers who are already highly skilled.

Does all this mean that we are heading towards a knowledge economy, where we will compete largely on high-skill, high-quality goods and services? Probably not. Not even Reich (1991) at his most optimistic anticipated that more than a minority of people would work in knowledge intensive jobs. Many occupations are routine and demand little of the workers who are employed in them. Automation provides opportunities for knowledge workers, but it also removes and deskills other jobs. It looks as though the broad labour market of low- and highly-skilled work is with us to stay.

4

Pay and Reward

What people are paid, how they are paid and, crucially, how much they are paid are key aspects of employment. Of course work is about more than money. The British Social Attitudes Survey asks its respondents whether they would work even if they did not need the money and every time this question is asked the majority of people confirm that they would, with 55 per cent of respondents agreeing in 2005 (BSAOnline, 2013). But just because work is about more than pay does not mean that pay is not important. It is. It enables workers to pay their rent, heat their houses, buy food, clothe themselves and their children and fund holidays. The amount a worker is paid will influence where they can live, whether they rent or buy and what sort of property they live in. It will shape hobbies, friendships and their children's prospects. This money may compensate them for giving up their time to their employer or reward them for demonstrating desirable behaviours and reaching specific targets.

This chapter provides an overview of pay. It starts by reviewing the basic ways people are paid – paying the job, paying for time, paying the person and paying for performance – before going on to consider a contentious aspect of HRM – Performance Related Pay (PRP). PRP rewards staff for their performance and was one of the original and distinctive pillars of HRM. In theory it wins widespread support, after all, who wouldn't agree with the proposition that those who contribute more should be rewarded? In practice it is incredibly difficult (some say impossible) to implement. We then go on to consider the people at either end of the pay and reward spectrum – the extremely highly paid and those whose pay is regulated by the National Minimum Wage (NMW) – as well as the gap that still persists between the pay that men receive and that awarded to women.

Pay

Pay can take the form of fixed amounts on the basis of *time* worked with hourly, weekly or monthly rates. Alternatively, employers can fund *performance* either by paying by results through piecework and commission, or by performance related increments to a basic salary. For both of these approaches the amounts involved can vary substantially and it is worth looking at what people in various occupations actually earn, from the high paid to those who earn the least. In 2015 UK MPs were paid a basic salary of £74,000 as well as a generous pension and a series of allowances to enable them to run an office, have houses in both London and their constituencies, and travel between the two. Junior doctors' salaries in the NHS start at £22,636, while consultants' range from £75,249 on first appointment to £101,451 after 19 years' experience, with up to an additional £75,796 available for those who rate a Platinum Clinical Excellence Award. At the other end of the scale ACP were paying their night cleaners £6.73 an hour, McDonald's crew members start at £7,580, call centre workers in Preston were being offered £12,231 plus a possible bonus of up to £4,000 and the AA was advertising call centre work at £16,730 plus an 'attractive' bonus. These are substantial differences in levels of pay, which materially affect workers' lives.

Paying for time and paying the job

The way that hourly, monthly or annual rates are set varies from job to job and employer to employer. Time-based payments are by far the simplest, and the most common, form of payment. Hourly, weekly or monthly rates are set; employers and employees both know the extent of their expected liabilities or income and can plan accordingly, and systems are straightforward to administer and control.

Within this, of course, different jobs attract different levels of pay. A number of elements can account for these variations including the skills and competencies the job holder exercises, their position in the hierarchy, the tasks that they perform and the responsibilities they have. Legacy is also important. Realistically most firms pay jobs particular amounts because they have always paid those jobs those amounts (suitably adjusted for inflation).

Formal processes do exist to rate jobs in terms of one another and the most commonly used are job evaluation schemes (Kessler, 2013). Non-analytic schemes simply rank jobs in relation to each other. Few provide any sort of rationale behind the rankings and raters may exercise their prejudices rather than looking at the substantive content of the jobs. These are rarely used since (unsurprisingly) they provide no defence against employment tribunals. Analytic job evaluation, by contrast, is a highly structured process. It focuses on the *job* rather than the *person*, disaggregates that job into a series of component parts, allocates scores for a range of activities such as personal skills, working conditions, physical capabilities and responsibilities, then adds up these individual

Table 4.1 Job evaluation weighting scheme, National Health Service *Agenda for Change*

	1	2	3	4	5	6	7	8
Communication	5	12	21	32	45	60		
Knowledge, training and experience	16	36	60	88	120	156	196	240
Analytical skills	6	15	27	42	60			
Planning/ organisational skills	6	15	27	42	60			
Physical skills	6	15	27	42	60			
Responsibility – patient care	4	9	15	22	30	39	49	60
Responsibility – policy/service	5	12	21	32	45	60		
Responsibility – finance/physical	5	12	21	32	45	60		
Responsibility – staff	5	12	21	32	45	60		
Responsibility – information	4	9	16	24	34	46		
Responsibility – research and development	5	12	21	32	45	60		
Freedom to act	5	12	21	32	45	60		
Physical effort	3	7	12	18	25			
Mental effort	3	7	12	18	25			
Emotional effort	5	11	18	25				
Working conditions	3	7	12	18	25			

Source: Managing human resources: human resource management in transition by Bach, S. and Edwards, M.R. (2013, p.130). Reproduced with permission of Wiley in the format 'Book' via Copyright Clearance Center.

scores in the hope of re-creating the whole job. Scores are generally based on observations of, and conversations with, job holders and the total score is used to allocate occupations to pay grades. Jobs are generally put into a pay band with several increments to allow a small amount of salary progression for experienced workers. Such increments are a form of deferred reward. They operate on the assumption that individuals are not fully competent on starting work so defer the point at which they are paid the full salary for their work until a few years in to their careers.

Table 4.1 shows the NHS's job evaluation weighting scheme (taken from Kessler, 2013). This allocates points for 16 different activities. The activities are not equally weighted. So, for example, communication can earn up to 60 points on the first six parts of the scale, but there are only four levels of reward for emotional effort which is capped at 25 points, as are physical effort, mental effort and working conditions. Only two criteria are assessed across the full eight columns of the scale: responsibility for patient care which can earn up to 60 points, and knowledge, training and experience, by far the most heavily weighted category, with up to 240 points to be gained, four times the next highest item on the scale. There are up to 1,000 points available and pay bands are allocated according to the totals earned, so healthcare assistants' jobs would gain them 161–270 points (with those on Band One earning £14,153–£17,253 and those on Band Two earning £16,110–£19,077) while nurses' work is scored between 326 and 465 points and can earn £21,176–£27,625 on Band Five progressing to £25,528–£34,189 on Band Six (Kessler, 2013).

Clearly job evaluation is not an exact science. Devising the criteria, observing them in action and scoring are all subjective and there are often questions about why one particular activity is deemed to outrank others. When universities went through the Higher Education Role Analysis process one institution chose to award higher scores for administrative staff working in the central functions than for those based in departments, since this university-wide view was felt to be more skilful. As a result, many very senior departmental staff, who undertook highly responsible work, were downgraded.

Job evaluations have been criticised. The points allocated to activities are matters of subjective judgement; points may be awarded in ways that are gendered, racialised or class-based. Jobs can be, and are, performed in very different ways. And it is not clear that de- and re-constructing occupations is the most effective way of capturing the nature of the job. They are probably primarily useful for internal comparisons (although the consultants who design them attempt to make them transferrable between organisations as well). In companies that have strong internal labour markets, like the civil service, these internal comparisons may well be most significant but in most organisations where recruitment is not confined to entry level positions and where workers may be lured away to rival firms on the promise of higher salaries, knowing about and adjusting to market pay rates does matter. Accordingly, most job evaluation systems include the idea of a 'market supplement' so the pay of jobs that are in demand can be upgraded. This is an extremely practical and necessary precaution for most firms and employment tribunals accept it as a legitimate reason for pay differentials, but having such a 'wild card' effectively preserves pay disparities regardless of the way work is evaluated.

Paying for performance

The main alternative to paying for time is paying for performance and this is the aspect of pay that HR writers and practitioners are most interested in. Traditional industrial relations and personnel textbooks would refer to pay as 'compensation', mitigating the unpleasant effects of work for workers. HRM textbooks label it 'reward' and try to devise ways that pay can be used strategically to motivate, encourage commitment and provide incentives. Set time-based rates are inadequate for this so the 'New Pay' (Lawler, 1990) associated with HRM is variable and aims to pay the *person* rather than the *job*.

This targets one of management's key dilemmas: that hiring someone to do a job does not guarantee that the job gets done, nor that it gets done in the way that management would like it done. So, rather than rewarding employees simply for turning up, as time-based payment systems do, variable payment systems separate out elements of work that are particularly vital to the employer (selling more cars, photocopiers or widgets; securing high customer satisfaction ratings; dealing with a high volume of work in a limited timescale) and allocates all or part of pay to these activities.

Such variations in pay have a long history. F.W. Taylor famously made piecework an integral part of Scientific Management so that workers would have an incentive to put effort in to their task (Taylor, 1949). Piecework is still widely used today. Fruit pickers may get paid for picking a specified weight of fruit, newspaper boys and girls are paid for each paper they deliver and home workers are paid for every porcelain model they paint. In general this type of payment is associated with low pay. Dutton and colleagues' (2008) study of hotel room attendants notes that the two hotels which paid piecework offered rates of £1.77 per room, with a target of cleaning 16 rooms in a five-hour shift and £2.47 per room with a target of 12 rooms in a six-hour shift. Since messy rooms could and did take longer to clean it is hardly surprising that many cleaners reported earning less than the minimum wage.

Other forms of variable pay supplement basic pay, rather than replacing it. These include merit awards, based on jobholders demonstrating a number of pre-set soft skills or behaviours; profit sharing schemes which distribute parts of a firm's profit to its workers in the form of cash or shares (generally encouraged by the tax officials and structured in tax efficient ways); and commission which links earnings to the number and type of items sold. But the area of pay which has attracted most attention from proponents of HRM is PRP. PRP schemes set a series of work-related targets for workers to achieve then rate their performance and pay out bonuses against those targets. It is a deliberate attempt to use the payment system to change behaviours, encouraging and rewarding ones the organisation is particularly interested in.

KFC, the fast food chain, has a PRP system for all staff with monthly targets and bonuses focused entirely on sales. Workers in restaurants which exceeded their sales targets received a £20 bonus (for achieving 105 per cent of sales, rising to £25 and £30 for 110 and 115 per cent, while team leaders received £10, £15 and £20 and there was a general team bonus of £5). Certificates celebrating performance were also given to outlets exceeding sales targets. Because awards were tied to sales the system was self-funding. In the first month of operation 26 per cent of staff were awarded bonuses, with 14 per cent of staff winning awards in the second month (IDS, 2013)

The principle of PRP schemes is simple: people who perform well are rewarded. It is a principle that most workers agree with. However, the practice is rarely as straightforward and most PRP schemes fail, or at least fail to produce the results their designers hoped for. There are a number of reasons for this and here we focus on five of the most significant: work is complicated and pay schemes can distort behaviour; performance criteria are difficult to devise; variable pay schemes are complicated and costly to administer; pay is not a motivator; and varying pay raises issues of equity.

The first problem, that *work is complicated and pay schemes can distort behaviour*, can be illustrated by taking the example of a primary school teacher. Most work involves a whole range of different tasks. Primary schools in Britain are currently assessed and put in league tables based on how well children perform in national tests (SATs) at two stages – Year two (ages six to seven) and Year six (ages ten to eleven) – so it would seem reasonable to award PRP based on scores in these tests. This data is publicly available, it is very easy to interpret and, since the tests are taken in May, class teachers will have had nearly nine months of teaching to help influence pupils' scores.

However, if teachers then (rationally) sought to win their bonuses, the system could create problems. Lessons would need to focus on the tests and rational teachers could neglect children who are comfortably at, above, or significantly below the appropriate level to concentrate their efforts on the ones just below, who have the potential to improve. Class time could be used for regular practice papers, with extra-curricular distractions firmly discouraged (even assuming that our teacher had any energy left to plan these). Not an attractive classroom, and we have not even started to express concerns about fraud (particularly in Year two when teachers mark their own class's SATs papers). Of course in reality our unfortunate class teacher is likely to be trying to achieve *both* the educational ideal of engaging children, supporting their social and emotional development *and* maximising the school's SATs performance.

PRP distorts behaviour since people focus on securing the proffered reward. This is, after all, the reason why PRP schemes are established, but securing the reward may require behaviours that distort and damage the job overall. A vivid example of this kind of perverse incentive stems from China under Chairman Mao. In order to combat an invasion of rats a provincial government offered a bounty for rats' tails to all citizens. The population responded enthusiastically and brought in rats' tails, and more rats' tails, and even more rats' tails but, although the government was now paying out significant amounts in rewards, the numbers of rats continued to rise. It turned out that the enterprising populace, realising that rats' tails had become a marketable commodity, had set up rat farms. Fans of Terry Pratchett's fantasy novels will be delighted to learn that the ever-astute Patrician, Lord Vetinari, had a solution to this. Learning of an infestation of rats in *Guards! Guards!* he responded, 'tax the rat farms' (Pratchett, 1989).

Few jobs are so straightforward that they can be totally encapsulated in a small number of simple performance criteria. Even sales work, ostensibly one of the most straightforward to assess and where commission-based payments have a long history, can be distorted. Inappropriate high pressure sales by banks resulted in the pensions mis-selling crisis of the 1990s and the payment protection insurance scandal of the 2010s. In both instances the financial institutions involved were fined heavily and required to make restitution.

Given this, it might seem that what is needed are better performance indicators. But, this brings us to the second issue, *performance criteria are difficult to devise*. According to the SMART acronym so widely used in the practitioner literature, criteria need to be specific, measurable, achievable, realistic and tangible. To be realistic objectives need to be straightforward to assess. But they also need to be meaningful to the organisation, equitable to the workers and have some resilience against attempts to 'game' the system. Since not everything that is important is measurable, and not everything that is measurable is important, this is a challenge. If you don't believe just how challenging it can be, try writing performance targets for a specific occupation, following the SMART acronym. Then swap your targets with an enterprising colleague and see if they can maximise their bonus payments. You will be amazed at the results. Set targets of arrests and police officers will enthusiastically book people for the most minor offences, sales staff can put pressure on customers to reach targets, workers can lie about performance and doctors dispense or withhold drugs with abandon. A target cannot take context or individual circumstances into account and criteria which seem perfectly sensible on the HR manager's desk or in a government department can have a devastating effect on the ground. Small wonder then that Cox (2000) dismisses all forms of performance related pay as unworkable.

The third issue is that *variable pay systems are complicated and expensive to administer.* Cox's (2005) study of small firms reveals just how costly and time consuming such systems could be. Consultants advised on implementation and were often called in repeatedly to check errors and remedy omissions; senior management time was taken up in extensive negotiations beforehand and dealing with problems once implemented; supervisors were required to sign off performance and attendance, sometimes on a daily basis, as well as conduct appraisals; payroll staff numbers were increased and were taken up with processing the various performance sheets and dealing with queries. This was a costly exercise and, since the dramatic increases in workload often left supervisors with little space to actually check on performance, and computerised records of factory output and employee productivity could not be aligned, there were no checks on workers' self-reports.

The fourth stumbling block is that *pay is not a motivator.* There is evidence that low pay actively *demotivates,* and some researchers extrapolated from this to argue that high pay, or differently structured pay, would motivate. But it is not clear that this necessarily follows. Indeed Herzberg (1993), in his classic text *Motivation to Work,* differentiates between 'motivators' and 'hygiene' factors, with pay clearly classified as a 'hygiene' factor. Hygiene factors are important, and need to be got right, because they can have significant demotivating effects, but they do not motivate. A nice example of this is heating. If you were working in an office in the middle of winter with freezing temperatures outside and the heating failed you would be likely to be demotivated and probably much too cold to work. It would certainly prompt complaints. But a heating system that worked perfectly would not have the opposite effect. After all, no-one ever felt motivated to work that extra bit harder because the temperature in their office was just right. When hygiene factors work well, they are not noticed. Herzberg argues that this is the case with pay. A badly designed payment system can result in a great deal of discontent. A well designed payment system may be an asset to an organisation, but it will not, of itself, motivate staff.

Finally, *varying pay also raises issues of equity.* Pay schemes which fail to differentiate between good and excellent performers, or which unfairly reward poor performers, can cause problems in the workplace. This places a considerable degree of responsibility on line managers, who are often the people required to monitor staff and appraise performance and staff may devote their attention to improving relationships with managers rather than focus on the job. Since firms are concerned that line managers may favour their own staff, or be overly generous in appraisal grades, many PRP schemes limit the number of positive awards they can make, and insist on a forced distribution of workers across all ratings, from unsatisfactory to outstanding. HBOS's system rewarded most workers, but always ensured that 5 per cent would get no increase in pay and a further 20 per cent would receive below inflation (Ellis and Taylor, 2010). It is easy to see why capping the number of outstanding awards is a practical and necessary step for an organisation to take, but, unsurprisingly such a move causes problems in the workplace, and problems with pay are felt particularly deeply.

Just how destructive such systems can be are evident in Microsoft's system of 'stack ranking' appraisals in which every business unit was forced to declare set proportions of their employees as top performers, average and poor. According to one former software developer:

> If you were in a team of ten people, you walked in the first day knowing that, no matter how good everyone was, two people were going to get a great review, seven were going to get mediocre reviews, and one was going to get a terrible review.

Pay, promotions and job security all depended on these ratings so high performing professionals avoided working with others who had good reputations, increasing attention was focused on appeasing supervisors and delivering short-term 'wins', and other internal projects were actively sabotaged. Innovations which staff dreamt up never made it beyond conception or prototypes and Microsoft entered a 'Lost Decade', decisively losing place in technology markets (Eichenwald, 2012).

Such feelings are not restricted to workers. Frans de Waal's zoological studies reveal that animals also object to unequal rewards. One short video, revealing just how annoyed a Capuchin monkey becomes when he receives only cucumber, while his neighbour is rewarded with (eminently more desirable) grapes is well worth watching (it can be seen at www.ted.com/talks/frans_de_waal_do_animals_have_morals.html). This is one extremely annoyed monkey.

Clearly not every PRP scheme is a disaster. Gilman (2013) notes the way schemes have increased output for piecework and commission-based sales and Marsden (2010) has argued that having a PRP system in place actually ensures that line managers complete appraisals and check up on their staff (although elsewhere both have revealed problems with schemes). However problems are widespread. Incentives can secure temporary changes in behaviour but these tend to reflect compliance rather than changes to underlying attitudes. There is no evidence that pay motivates and considerable evidence that low pay or problematic payment systems actually *de*motivate. Incentives, not unnaturally, make workers focus on the incentive rather than the job, workplace relations can be spoiled since colleagues will now be competitors and superiors need to be placated to secure good appraisals. Rewards discourage self-directed behaviour and taking responsibility for the whole job; they also discourage managers from managing (except around the area of pay).

Most performance related pay schemes cover only a small propor-tion of pay. Arrowsmith and colleagues' (2010) study of variable pay schemes in four countries reveals schemes generally capped at a small proportion of the wage bill (typically between 1 and 4 per cent, with one offering as much as 10 per cent of the wage bill). Another way of putting this into perspective is to check how many workers are eligi-ble to *receive* some sort of performance related pay or payment by results and the answer, again, is a small minority. More than three-quarters of all workers, and 93 per cent of public sector workers, are paid only fixed pay and, while 54 per cent of workplaces report some kind of incentive pay scheme (merit pay, performance related pay, payment by results, profit related pay or share schemes) the majority restrict these to managerial employees: 84 per cent of workplaces which have performance related pay schemes for their managers provide no equivalent incentives for the non-managerial staff (van Wanrooy et al., 2013: 24–25).

Of course, pay does not have to be officially 'flexible' in order to be changed, indeed adjustments to pay (upwards to compensate for the effect of inflation, downwards when an employer is struggling to pay or as an alternative to redundancies) are a regular feature of working life. The 2011 UK Workplace Employment Relations Study was con-ducted during a private sector recession (the public sector recession followed just after the data had been collected) and, while there had been limited redundancies, pay adjustments were reported by a sig-nificant number of respondents with 33 per cent reporting that their pay had been frozen or cut, 29 per cent that the workload had increased (14 per cent had both their workload increased *and* their pay cut) and 19 per cent that access to overtime was restricted. On occa-sion the recession may have been an excuse for action rather than a spur with 54 per cent of employees located in workplaces that were *not* affected by the recession reporting changes to pay or terms and conditions (van Wanrooy et al., 2013: 8).

It is easy to see why PRP is such a popular part of HRM. It seems to offer managers the power to ensure not only that work is done, but that it is done in the way the organisation would like, and to the time-scale the organisation sets. This however, is an idea that is great in theory and a disaster in practice. Most firms seem to tacitly acknowledge this, offering PRP in limited amounts for small proportions of the workforce.

High pay and executive rewards

One significant feature of pay over the last few decades is the way that it has polarised, with the lowest paid stagnating and the highest paid 'flying' ahead (Kessler, 2013). This is particularly marked in the USA where pay for the bottom 10 per cent of wage-earners has flat-lined since the 1980s, resulting in real term cuts to standards of living (Green, 2006). According to Bebchuck and Fried (2004), in 1991 the average US CEO received 140 times the pay of an average worker and by 2003 this ratio was 500:1. In the UK, executive pay has risen to the extent that the average pay packet for a FTSE-100 CEO is £4.6m a year (Boffey, 2016).

The timing of some of these awards is unfortunate. In 2012 HSBC, the UK's biggest bank, made £13.7 billion in profits (down 6 per cent from the year before). Its chief executive was well rewarded for his contribution, with earnings and bonuses totalling £10 million and 204 staff earned over £1 million each. But those further down the hierarchy were not paid quite so generously for their service with some staff earning as little as £14,000 a year. Nor were profits invested in improving terms and conditions overall. During the year the bank had made 27,000 staff redundant, had reduced the holiday entitlement by two days and was changing the staff pension scheme, effectively reducing members' benefits. Shortly after these announcements it decided to make a further tranche of people redundant, or, as HSBC put it in their press release, staff were 'demised' (Treanor, 2013). Morrisons' CEO Dalton Phillips nearly doubled his remuneration to £2.1m in the year before he was sacked (Boffey, 2016) and Sir Fred Goodwin, CEO of the Royal Bank of Scotland, earned over £4m the year before the bank collapsed then walked away with a pension of over £700,000 a year (Kessler, 2013). Everything that an organisation does sends messages to its staff, customers and shareholders. The generous rewards available to those at the top, apparently without regard to organisational performance, have been extensively criticised and even the corporate head-hunters responsible for the majority of boardroom appointments have protested that pay levels for most senior executives were 'absurdly high' with CEOs themselves 'mediocre' rather than exceptional. It seems likely though that such awards will continue since all also went on to confirm that they would not advise a client to ask for less money, since this sent the wrong signals to the appointing committee (Boffey, 2016).

The explanation for these awards is not exemplary performance or extensive responsibilities but, quite simply, bargaining power (Bebchuck and Fried, 2004). CEOs win such large pay awards because they can, with awards decoupled from performance and contractual payoffs for redundancies or ends of contract. Shareholders have limited power to intervene. It seems that over-inflated executive pay, while deeply unpopular, is with us to stay.

Low pay and the National Minimum Wage

While very few people enjoy the sort of financial rewards secured by the CEOs of large companies, a significant minority at the other end of the pay spectrum count as low paid. There is no single definition of low pay. Some studies propose set amounts based on purchasing power and baskets of commodities, setting levels below which people would struggle to pay rent or buy food and clothing; others suggest that low pay is relative and define it as a proportion of the average wage. One commonly accepted definition, seen in the Council of Europe's standard of decency, is that low pay is two-thirds of average (mean) earnings in an economy (Rubery and Edwards, 2003). In 2005 25 per cent of the US workforce was in low-wage work, together with 22 per cent in the UK, 21 per cent in Germany, 18 per cent in the Netherlands, 13 per cent in France and 8.5 per cent in Denmark (Solow, 2008: 6). The US, UK and German figures are all worryingly high, and vividly demonstrate the pay gap between these workers and the well-paid CEOs.

In 1997 the incoming Labour government introduced a National Minimum Wage to the UK, setting a floor below which pay could not legally fall. The initial rate was set prudently low, at £3.60 an hour for workers over 21, about half average wages at the time. This was intended to provide meaningful support for workers, while remaining affordable for businesses, particularly those in cleaning, security and social care where wages are a high proportion of costs. When it was introduced, this rate covered just under 10 per cent of the workforce. The rate has risen every year and in March 2016 was £6.70 for workers over 21, with the rate for under 18s £3.87 and £3.30 for apprentices.

There is a clear moral argument for introducing minimum wage legislation. Employees have less bargaining power than employers, and employees who are paid low wages have considerably less bargaining power. Given such a disparity, some employers can and do force pay rates down below subsistence levels. One example that George Bain, first head of the Low Pay Commission, was fond of quoting was an advert for a security guard offering pay of £1 an hour. The security guard was required to bring their own dog. As Winston Churchill argued when wages councils (Trade Boards) were introduced in 1909:

> where you have what we call sweated trades, you have no organisa-tion, no parity of bargaining, the good employer is undercut by the bad, and the bad employer is undercut by the worst

In order to safeguard workers' interests, and ensure that they and their families are able to survive, governments need to support wage legislation.

Set against this is the problem of whether employers will be able to afford to pay whatever rates are set and whether the existence of mini-mum wages will damage businesses. Traditionally this was an argument conducted by economists who argued that firms paid workers what they could afford (the rate at the intersection of the supply and demand curves), and that artificially increasing pay would result in unemploy-ment and bankruptcies, since businesses would not be able to afford to employ people. Card and Krueger's (1995) research challenged this. They studied minimum wage legislation in the USA, where decisions are taken at federal level and states with minimum wage legislation may be located next to those with no such regulation. They found that, where rates were set prudently low, employment actually increased. Low-paid workers are more likely to spend their wage increases, boosting the local economy, and people who might otherwise have found it uneco-nomic to work are tempted back into the labour market. In the UK, where the economy has been extensively and repeatedly studied for the slightest negative impact following the NMW legislation, the only evi-dence of concern is from the care sector, a labour intensive, low-wage industry, and even this is limited.

On the positive side, over this period about 10 per cent of the work-force have benefitted from the NMW, earning about 20 per cent more than they would have (Deakin and Green, 2009; Kessler, 2013). This has made a significant difference to their standard of living. The benefi-ciaries have disproportionately been women, ethnic minorities, part-timers, home workers, young workers and lone parents.

Spurred on by the success of the NMW but alarmed by the fact that many people earning at the minimum level could not afford to live and work in most of the UK a *Living Wage Campaign* (www.livingwage.org. uk/about-living-wage) began. Living Wage rates are set independently against the price of a basket of goods and services and represent the cost of living in the UK. In 2016 it was set at £9.40 an hour for London and £8.25 an hour for the rest of the country. Participation is voluntary but according to the campaign's website 45,000 families have already been lifted out of poverty by the scheme and the organisations which have adopted it have reported improvements to work quality as well as reduced absenteeism and turnover. The 2012 London Olympics were the first ever Living Wage Olympics and many high profile employers signed up to the cause. But the scheme is a voluntary one and most employers do not pay living wages. These include the government. In November 2012 when one of the cleaners working in the government offices in Downing Street left a polite note asking the Deputy Prime Minister, Nick Clegg to support the Living Wage Campaign he was rapidly disciplined, had his salary reduced by £400 a month when his overtime was taken away, and was moved to another site by his employers.

Confusingly, the Conservative government was so taken with the term Living Wage that it adopted it in place of the NMW, introducing a new higher rate of £7.20 an hour for workers over 25 on 1 April 2016 (the National Living Wage, NLW). Unfortunately they did not also adopt the Living Wage Campaign principle of setting the rate at the level a worker needed to earn in order to live and the government NLW rate was considerably lower than the voluntary Living Wage (who planned to rename themselves the Real Living Wage). The rise in minimum wage rates was welcome, but this was not a living wage.

The gender pay gap

We noted above that women workers disproportionately benefitted from the NMW in the UK. The main reason for this is that women are paid less than men. Indeed women are in a majority in 11 of the 15 lowest paid occupations, while conversely, men are over-represented in 11 of the 15 highest paid occupations (Perfect, 2012). In 1970 the UK passed the Equal Pay Act, making it a legal requirement for employers to pay women and men the same rates for work of equal value. Until that point many employers had set separate, lower, rates for women workers with payscales offering differential pay for skilled, unskilled and women workers, with the lowest rates for women.

Despite the fact that this legislation has existed for nearly half a century there is a still a gap between women's pay and men's. For full-time workers the gap was 13.9 per cent in 2015 and on 9 November the Fawcett Society celebrated Equal Pay Day since that was the point from which women workers would be effectively working for free until the end of the year (http://www.fawcettsociety.org.uk/our-work/campaigns/ equal-pay-day-2/). The gap is greatest for part-time work, and stood at 39 per cent in 2012 (Perfect, 2012: 3).

The classical economic arguments are that women workers are paid less because they invest less in their working lives. They may take career breaks or move to part-time work to care for young children or elderly parents. They are less well qualified than men, opt for different subjects in school and college and select different occupations when working. There is some truth in this. Women bear a disproportionate share of household and caring responsibilities (Hochschild and Machung, 2003) and they are more likely to work part-time. However, we should not under-estimate the role of prejudice and discrimination. In higher education today there are more women than men. The gender wage gap is falling (Lindley, 2005) but, as the Fawcett Society point out, at the current rate of progress it will take 50 years to reach equality. And even studies of recent graduates confirm a pay gap (Purcell and Elias, 2004).

Discussion and conclusions

Pay is an important aspect of work. It is, after all, the reason why most people work and it shapes the way workers live. A great deal of academic effort has gone into examining the way that pay is delivered and determined, whether it is assessed by time, or skills, or performance, or responsibilities, or qualifications, or experience, or contribution. As noted above, while time-based payment systems may be unfashionable, they are easily understood, simple to administer and meet demands for equity more readily than many other schemes. They are also by far the most widely used payment systems.

Contingent payment systems, including PRP, have attracted a lot more attention and have a far greater propensity to go wrong. Many of the problems with these systems have been considered above but it is worth stressing the issue of equity here. Systems that are felt to be unfair can create a lot of problems for management. Following the banking crisis of 2008 Ellis and Taylor reported on ordinary bank staff who had been given shares as part of their pay (2010: 806, 807):

> Since the 1990s staff have often taken part of their salary increase in shares or indeed all of it, after all there was a tax incentive to do so. It would not be uncommon for somebody working in the back office who had £3,000 in a bonus to think, 'I'm going to put some of that into shares.' It is not uncommon for somebody working as a teller on

£15,000 to £18,000, who's been with the company for 15 years, to have built up £20,000 in shares. Most people thought that anyone who didn't buy into these schemes was crazy because it seemed that you were, you know, why wouldn't you? Based on their own experience the share prices had only gone up for a number of years ... When the HBOS share price began to go down, nobody believed that it would collapse, it was at £11 and then to go to £9, £8 ... Staff couldn't believe that had happened but people did still had a feeling that they trusted their employer. Nobody sold their shares because they all thought that it would go back up. The message we got from senior management on a weekly basis was 'this is a strong bank, today we have held a meeting with our most significant investors, and we have told them, we have told the City, this is a strong bank. We have a strong asset base.' People really watched in disbelief – and I do mean watched, because the share price was on the intranet and they could watch it daily, live, every 15 minutes – as they began to lose their savings. I would need to recalculate but in early May 2009 whatever you had in shares were worth 2 percent of what they were 18 months ago.

Understandably staff felt hurt, angry, shocked and betrayed. Junior staff with no control over bank strategies lost most of their savings in the crisis and many also lost their jobs. The downside of contingent pay schemes, and of pay schemes where bonuses are based on shares, is the risk of price collapse.

In tandem with this, executive pay has soared, often very publicly, to levels that not even executive head-hunters can defend. Given how important equity is within firms this has clear implications for internal dissent. At the other end of the spectrum significant proportions of workers count as low-paid. The NMW has done a great deal to protect UK workers and the introduction of the National Living Wage has raised the rate for workers over 25 but this is not actually a living wage and there is more that could be done.

5

Flexible Work and Flexible Workers

For many people the traditional idea of work is a little like something from a black and white film. A man, in a suit and tie, probably also wearing a bowler hat, is employed in an office. Alternatively we can substitute the tie and bowler hat for overalls and imagine our worker in a factory, hurrying to the gates in company with large numbers of other workers in order to clock in, then rushing out thankfully at the end of the shift. These images are out of date by at least 50 or 60 years. The workplaces they conjure up are very different and our imaginary workers are likely to have had varying experiences in them but they shared a number of common features. Work was full time and permanent with the public sector and many of the large bureaucracies such as banks offering jobs for life (at least for male employees). Hours of work were stable, or, given the topic of this chapter, *inflexible*, and often shared with other workers, so office staff might be expected to be at their desks from 9 am to 5 pm, while factory workers were employed on agreed shifts.

These are images that might best describe the generation in employment after 1945. Until that point, for many, if not most workers, work was insecure. After 1945 many white collar (office) workers benefitted from lifetime employment, blue collar workers in the factories did indeed experience redundancy but this tended to coincide with the economic cycle so they were hired when orders required more workers and fired when there was no work for them to do. Unions protected workers' rights, working hours were controlled, health and safety legislation helped to create safer workplaces, salary levels and pension provision grew and contracts tended to be secure. Such a system had a number of advantages for workers: earnings were predictable; many also had pensions to safeguard them from poverty in old age; and they were often protected from arbitrary redundancy. In exchange for loyalty from workers, employers offered loyalty in return. Of course, not all workers were quite so privileged. Migrants, like my father, were often excluded from union membership, hired on lower rates of pay than British-born workers and were the first to be fired when the economy was difficult. Women were also excluded from full labour market privileges, paid less, and often required to give up work on marriage. But many full-time, male, British-born workers did enjoy secure and stable employment.

In the 1980s this started to change. With right-wing governments on both sides of the Atlantic the focus in the UK shifted from safeguarding workers' rights, given the imbalance of power in the employment relationship, to providing firms with more flexibility, so they did not have to spend money on workers they did not need. Atkinson (1984), one of the early writers on flexibility, put forward a model to explain how this would affect companies. In his *Flexible Firm* key tasks are still performed by full-time workers employed on secure, permanent contracts (the organisational 'core') but tasks which are less central to organisational survival, or which are required only infrequently, are undertaken by people employed on 'flexible', insecure contracts. So a new computer system might be designed and installed by IT consultants hired for that specific project, additional administrative staff could be brought in through a temporary employment agency to assist with the clerical work at the busiest times of year, and cleaning could be outsourced with

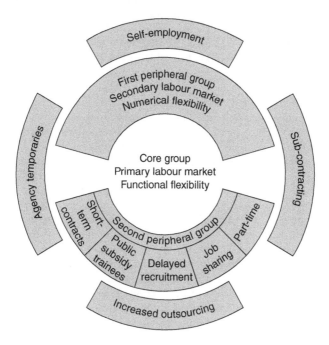

Figure 5.1 The flexible firm model

Source: Atkinson, J. 1984. 'Manpower strategies for flexible organisations.' *Personnel Management* August: 28–31. Reproduced with the permission of the publisher, the Chartered Institute of Personnel and Development, London (www.cipd.co.uk).

offices maintained by cleaners working for an entirely different company. In this model the factor that distinguishes between the core and each of the various peripheries is the centrality of the task to the organisation's survival. This is flexibility as a strategic option, designed around organisational activities.

If the media image of the secure workers of the 1950s and 1960s are bowler-hatted clerks and blue collar factory workers all hurrying to work at the same time, that of today's flexible workers is of attractive young professionals, armed with the latest in smartphones and tablets at liberty to do their challenging and highly remunerated projects in cafés, on golden beaches and in parks. These are workers freed from the rush hour commute, unfettered by office routines and blessed with permanently good weather. They can take a break to go to the gym during the day instead of competing for space after office hours, meet friends for lunch or simply relax. Because they are in control of their own schedules, work can be reorganised to times that fit in with life. It is a great image and it does capture some aspects of flexible work, but only some. As an academic I can work flexibly. When I teach and attend meetings I need to be on university premises at stated hours. But I also hold meetings around my kitchen table or in cafés, write in the office I have set up at home in my attic, read dissertations on trains and edit journal articles in hotel rooms. I enjoy a great deal of flexibility. For academics, though, this is nothing new and it is not reflected in our employment contracts. Professors who worked long before the internet was even thought of might not have been able to access e-mails from home (or trains, or cafés), but they would certainly recognise the meetings around the kitchen table, the office at home and all the reading and writing. They would also recognise my employment contract, which is traditional, full-time and permanent. Flexibility certainly exists in the workplace and some highly skilled workers are able to enjoy both secure contracts and the ability to work flexibly in ways that are convenient to them, but this is not the whole flexibility story. For many workers flexibility means flexibility for the employer rather than the employee, with working hours and schedules varying from week to week, low wages, anti-social hours and no guaranteed work.

In this chapter we will consider the various different kinds of flexibility. We look at temporary employment agencies, part-time work, zero hours contracts, contractors and freelancers and we consider the implications of each of these types of work for both employees and employers. Some are indeed highly skilled and well rewarded and we look at the IT specialists in Silicon Valley who enjoy the freedoms that contracting gives them (although few take advantage of it to increase their leisure hours or take their work to the nearest beach). However, these are very much in the minority. Many other flexible contracts are taken, disproportionately, by women, ethnic minorities and migrants, the people who have least labour market power and who work for low wages. These contracts also raise problems for employers over skill development, managing a workforce where people are employed on different terms and conditions and where staff are paid different rates for doing the same job.

Flexible work and flexible workers

Flexibility can include a wide range of working practices. The most common is the use of 'contingent' or 'precarious' contracts, employing people for work that is not a traditional permanent, full-time job. Such contracts provide employers with what Atkinson called *numerical flexibility* and the vast majority of employers use at least one form of flexibility and sub-contract at least one service. Numerical flexibility enables firms to respond to changing conditions by varying the number of people they employ. So, for example, a firm which hires call centre staff from a temporary employment agency can decide on a daily basis how many it requires and what hours it wishes to hire them for. Agency staff are not guaranteed work, although they often guarantee their availability: they may be texted or called in the morning and asked to go into work or not be called at all because no work is available.

Firms can also gain from *financial flexibility*. Instead of paying workers a regular wage payments can be contingent. So workers may get bonuses when the company has been particularly profitable, be paid piece rates for the number of items they make or commission for each sale that they secure (for more on this see Chapter 4). Finally, *functional flexibility* involves multi-skilling rather than the power to hire and fire workers at will. Under a system of functional flexibility firms' responsiveness stems from the fact that workers can perform more than one set of tasks. This is perhaps best exemplified by the way large Japanese firms employed and developed their male staff. Japanese firms would move workers from department to department exposing them to a range of employment practices. Lifetime employment was guaranteed and, rather than specialising in functional silos, employees gained a wide knowledge of the organisation as a whole.

Each type of flexibility has very different implications for people in work and those who hire them. In this chapter, we focus on *numerical flexibility*. This is the most common type of flexibility; low- and high-skilled workers are increasingly hired on contingent contracts. These used to be called *atypical* since the assumption was that a typical contract was permanent and full-time but given their increasing numbers, the term is no longer accurate.

Contingent work

Contingent or flexible work covers a wide range of employment contracts with very different levels of security, reward and career prospects for the job holders. These include part-time contracts, agency, outsourced and sub-contracted work and are often associated with lower wages and poorer terms and conditions than full-time, permanent contracts, indeed the largest gender pay gap is between men working full-time and women employed part-time (see Chapter 4). In this section we consider part-time work, agency work and outsourced work.

Part of the rationale for contingent contracts is that the employees take some of the risks associated with the employment relationship from the employer. Temporary employment agencies are one way of doing this. These link employers with employees. They are generally private sector companies (although the NHS in the UK also runs a temporary employment agency, set up in an attempt to save agency costs on some of the many temporary staff they employ). Such agencies can provide staff for short-term projects but they may also be used as a way of screening potential permanent employees or as a source of long-term temporary workers. Agency staff can be hired and fired at will. If an employer needs one (or a hundred) members of staff for an additional day, week or month's work they tell the agency and the agency call round the hopeful temps registered on their books. In this relationship the financial risk is taken by the worker, with most taken on highly insecure 'at will' contracts where the contract can be ended at minimal notice. Temps are required to be available and ready to work at a moment's notice, but there is no obligation on the employer to hire them. One worker, interviewed by Forde (2001), who had temped for three months, had had 20 different assignments, only one of which had lasted longer than a week. This is not to argue that employers did not value workers who knew their organisations and were familiar with their systems and staff, they did, and 'repeat' workers were highly prized by both agencies and their clients, but neither expected to pay extra or offer additional employment security in exchange for this.

Zero hours contracts are another way in which employers transfer risks to employees. In these, workers have a standard employment contract with their employer, so they enjoy some security of contract, but they are not guaranteed any work. Most firms avoid such contracts, with only 8 per cent of employers offering zero hours contracts in 2011, but the numbers are growing and this figure had doubled over the previous seven years (van Wanrooy et al., 2013: 10). This security of employment, but not of hours, is particularly common in retail. Large supermarkets employ many part-time staff on a variety of shift patterns, regularly moving people from one shift to another often at short notice, with shifts not announced until shortly before they start, and hours increased or reduced to fit the supermarket's requirements. Burger King, a fast food outlet in the UK, tried a more extreme version of this. When restaurants were quiet managers ordered staff to clock out, move to the other side of the counter and wait. When a customer came in they could clock back on and move behind the counter again. They were not paid for the time they spent waiting on the customers' side of the counter. An employment tribunal ruled against Burger King and required them to pay the workers for their full shifts. While this extreme example of exploitation was successfully prevented, the variations in hours and shifts experienced by the supermarket staff is still common practice.

Unsurprisingly, given this transfer of risk, many types of contingent work are undertaken by workers disadvantaged in the labour market. Reskin and Roos (1990) argue that there are 'queues' in the labour market, which follow workers' social status, rather than their skills, or educational qualifications, or expertise, so women, ethnic minorities and migrant workers (among others) are disadvantaged. Such 'queues' are apparent in a good deal of contingent work, where many members of disadvantaged groups are employed in considerable numbers. Just under 74 per cent of the part-time workers in the UK are women (6.15 of 8.35 million workers – ONS, 2015b: 1, 8); hotel room cleaners, employed part-time or on temporary agency contracts, are often immigrant women (Dutton et al., 2008); many migrants find themselves in poorly paid, low-skilled jobs (Ciujupius, 2011); migrant labour is extensively used in agriculture to harvest fruits where the work cannot be mechanised; and BME women are far more likely to be part of the emotional proletariat, working in low-paid service sector jobs (see Chapter 7).

When dealing with these disadvantaged workers employers may be fulsome in their praise, but this enthusiasm seldom translates into pay awards. Moss and Tilly (2001) in a detailed study of US employers, found many who were very positive about their migrant employees: they praised their work ethic, their commitment and their capacity for hard work. However, this praise always came with a financial penalty – the much valued migrants were paid 39 cents less per hour than their US-born colleagues when one manager in the organisation praised their work ethic and 96 cents less when more than one manager spoke up (2001: 117). These recruiters are not alone in preferring migrant labour.

MacKenzie and Forde report on one employer who, like Moss and Tilly's respondents, valued migrant labour highly (2009: 150):

> Their attitude to work is tremendous. If we wanted them to they'd work 24 hours a day seven days a week ... They are a very good workforce. 90 percent foreign ... This is the best the workforce has been since I have been here – 15 years.

This company, as a matter of policy, targeted vulnerable workers as employees. They started with local women and young men, before moving to migrants, switching their preferred nationalities to more recent entrants every time their existing workers became established in the labour market.

The BBC's documentary series *Inside Out* (BBC, 2015) highlighted some of the abuses experienced by vulnerable workers when they investigated working practices in a Sports Direct warehouse in Derbyshire. There, a casual workforce of around 3,500 mainly East Europeans were employed around the clock picking, packing and despatching orders. Announcements over the tannoys in the warehouse urged workers to greater efforts and the company ran a 'four strikes and you're out' system with 'strikes' earned for taking time off sick, chatting to co-workers or asking for a drink of water during a shift. Security guards regularly found bottles of urine in the warehouse, left by workers who had felt unable to take time away from their station to go to the toilet and both hand and ankle injuries were common when hard-pushed workers became trapped between cages. More seriously, in the two years before the BBC's investigation, ambulances had been called to the site 76 times, with almost half of these calls for patients with life-threatening conditions. Most workers spoke little English and put up with harsh management, health-threatening targets and being forced to work while sick because they feared unemployment. As Chris Forde argued, when workers are employed by agencies, rather than by an employer directly, the employer's aggression is likely to be amplified by the agency. Indeed one, Best Connection, boasted in its staff magazine that it had won the Sports Direct contract by 'closely monitoring the workforce and improving attendance'.

Outsourcing – transferring work to a specialist supplier, a different part of the country or to a different country – transfers even more of the risk away from the employer. In recent years outsourcing has increased dramatically. Improvements to technology, communication and transport have made it easier to shift production, and elements of production, yet still retain control over it. Expanding markets and relaxing trade barriers make such developments more attractive and the existence of highly skilled and low-wage workers allow employers to cut costs (Doellgast and Gospel, 2013). Approaches to outsourcing vary. Japanese companies have strong relationships with their supply chains and often share expertise and good practices over extended periods of time; German companies may try to extend good HR practices to outsourced client and customer organisations. However, in the USA and the UK such relationships tend to be more distant and many outsourcing decisions are taken in order to secure efficiency gains and cost savings. This is particularly true of decisions, such as that taken by Dyson to outsource production to the developing world, where wages are far lower.

Some organisations are so concerned with keeping costs down while maintaining the quality of their products that they are prepared to countenance serious abuses of workers' rights. Apple Computers have a particularly poor reputation in this area. They outsource iPad and iPhone assembly to Foxconn in China. Chan (2013) reports on the work experiences of one worker employed in a Foxconn assembly plant, Tian Yu. At the age of 17, after only 37 days of employment at the factory, Tian Yu threw herself from the fourth floor of her dormitory. It was 2010 and she was one of 18 Foxconn workers to attempt suicide that year. All were young, the oldest was only 25. She, and three others, survived, but all had crippling injuries. In her time at Foxconn Tian Yu worked 12-hour shifts, with only one day off each fortnight. Team meetings and roll calls were unpaid and held outside working hours, breaks were limited, tasks timed to the second and supervision was intense. Workers who made mistakes would be publicly humiliated, forced to stand at attention for hours or read self-critical statements of their errors to their co-workers. Tian Yu's monthly wage for this was about £140, including overtime. When an administrative error meant that her pay was sent to the wrong Foxconn factory she spent a day unsuccessfully trying to correct the mistake. She could not. Trapped in a dormitory with girls who did not speak her dialect, her mobile phone broke and she was unable to contact her family. Despairing, she attempted suicide. She survived, but ended up paralysed. In response, Foxconn attempted to introduce an anti-suicide clause in their employment contracts. This was dropped after a public outcry and the company did raise wages, but it also increased its production targets, increased working hours and kept the Taylorised work process with its humiliating punishments. Such low wages and working conditions are not restricted to China. In India the average wage for a garment worker in 2012 was about £39 a month, an amount that would barely cover food and rent (Jenkins, 2015: 202).

Outsourcing production enables organisations to take advantage of (often) highly skilled and committed workforces in developing countries who can be hired at far lower rates of pay than those in developed nations. It can also enable them to escape from their duty of care to these workers, since they are no longer the employer, with oppressive workplace regimes and serious breaches to health and safety countenanced.

High-skilled contingent work

Many of these problems – the transfer of risk, low pay and oppressive working conditions – have been observed when low-paid and low-skilled workers are hired on contingent contracts. With highly skilled workers there is still a transfer of risk. A firm may hire a management consultant or an IT specialist or a professional trainer to solve a specific problem, undertake a project or teach a course, but when that work (or the contract period) is finished they no longer need to take any responsibility for the worker they hired; however, because highly skilled workers tend to be highly paid, they are more likely to have funds available to cushion any gaps in employment. For these highly skilled contingent workers, contracts are about both obtaining work and ensuring that their skills are maintained, developed or stretched.

One professional group which includes considerable numbers of contingent workers is that of IT specialists and Barley and Kunda's (2004) study focuses on professional IT contractors in Silicon Valley. None had begun their career on contingent contracts. All had started in standard, full-time work but, following redundancies, downsizing and contracting out, took work as contractors. This was generally very well paid (which could cause resentment from the permanent staff) but came with no fringe benefits so pensions, holiday pay and medical insurance usually had to be funded by the contractors themselves. The work varied, as the contractors did, from highly skilled but dull routine tasks to 'bleeding edge' work, described as so far beyond the cutting edge it hurts both contractor and employer when it goes wrong. These differences in work could be seen in the various terms that employers used to describe their contractors, including gurus, warm bodies, pros, bottom feeders, consultants, contractors, specialists, generalists, seniors and juniors (2004: 64).

Firms hired contractors for a number of reasons: 'gurus' could teach employees skills that they did not have in-house; restrictions on headcount or limited budgets might impede hiring permanent workers (although since consultants were generally paid more than permanent staff this was often a matter of shuffling payments from one budget to another); employers might have struggled to fill key positions; skills might only be required for a short period and the contracting time could even be used to screen potential future employees. Employing significant numbers of contractors could even inflate a company's stock price since productivity was calculated as a ratio of full-time employees and contractors were easier to bury in the budget.

Individual contractors were responsible for their own skills development, an area that was both difficult and important since their opportunities for future work depended on knowledge of particular systems and software packages. Most sought 'stretchwork' in their assignments, which would hone and develop their skills. Some employers were prepared to trust contractors, experienced in other areas, to learn new skills at their expense, others allowed them to 'piggy back' new skills on work that they could already do, or negotiated lower rates because contractors were learning on the job.

To a certain extent, these are the workers that the enthusiastic work futurologists are thinking about when they describe knowledge workers who move between interesting, highly remunerated projects with ample leisure time to share with family and friends or indulge in exciting hobbies (see, for example Handy, 1990). The image of attractive young professionals working in parks or on beaches then taking time out to go to the gym that we presented at the start of the chapter, is closer to these knowledge workers than it is to the low-skilled temps employed on minimum wages. Barley and Kunda's informants were aware of this and enjoyed the freedoms that contracting gave them. All cited the advantages of controlling their own work and schedules, none wanted to return to standard permanent contracts, but, in reality there was an intriguing discrepancy between what contractors said and what they did with few taking advantage of their freedom to spend more time with family or indulge in hobbies. Almost all worked long hours and tried to avoid 'downtime' by hunting for new contracts when their existing ones ended through online bulletin boards, personal networks and professional agencies, with some contractors signed up with as many as 50 different agencies. One informant did use the freedom contracting offered to spend more time with their family and another made time for long distance yachting but these were the exceptions, rather than the rule. For most, contracting meant long hours and few breaks.

These contractors were fortunate. The demand for their services was high and, although they needed to put effort into regular job hunting, since contracts averaged only about seven months, most reported little 'downtime'. In UK film and TV production the oversupply of labour is significant with many professionals employed for about a third of the year and forced to find other ways of supplementing their income. Here too social networks advertise posts, facilitate recruitment and guarantee competence but in this labour market hiring via social networks favours white, middle-class professionals (Grugulis and Stoyanova, 2012).

So far we have observed a line between different types of flexibility that conforms to skill with highly skilled freelance contractors and low-skilled outsourced, temporary and often part-time work. This line is not always so simple. In the UK there has been a significant growth in highly skilled part-time work for women (largely fuelled by professional workers asking for part-time contracts when they return from maternity leave). Outsourced and sub-contracted work may also be highly skilled and Brown and colleagues' (2011) book, *The Global Auction* reveals how professional work such as writing legal briefs, interpreting medical investigations, research and development, and IT is being outsourced to the developing world. There, very highly skilled professionals can match the quality of service but at much lower rates of pay. There is no simple division between the 'hand' work, of repetitive routine assembly, and 'head' work of innovation and research and development, with routine work outsourced while innovation remains the preserve of the developed world. Rather, both are being outsourced. For the developing world this brings in much appreciated higher salaries, for the developed world it means a race to the bottom in terms of salary negotiations. China and India in particular have geared up to compete in this market for high value goods at breakneck speed.

Managing flexibility

Even when flexible forms of labour are used, the original employer still retains responsibility for ensuring that the tasks performed, goods produced, and services delivered meet appropriate standards of quality and timeliness. This has implications for management. When staff are employed in-house on varying contracts then management need to cope with organising teams of people who are aware that others are paid different rates of pay, with varying levels of security and access to benefits. Call centres may employ staff hired on a range of different pay rates, influenced more by client preferences than the nature of the work (Rubery et al., 2004). Barley and Kunda (2004) note that contractors earned significantly more than core staff. Set against this they often did not have access to staff computer systems, were positioned in the least desirable offices (which they often had to share) and might not have access to staff spaces, canteens or shared amenities. Differentiation which, understandably, causes comment on both sides.

When work is outsourced or sub-contracted management are still responsible for the services and goods produced, but they are no longer the employer. So disciplining agency nurses, addressing the poor skills of temporary workers or expressing concerns about absence are likely to involve others in cumbersome and time consuming processes. Monitoring work may also increase layers of management. One housing benefit department, which outsourced its work, had to retain specialist staff in-house to check every case approved by the outsourced caseworkers, work which was both onerous and tedious (Grugulis et al., 2003).

Barley and Kunda's (2004) contractors reported that communication was difficult, relations with permanent staff often not easy and both sides feared incompetence with contractors stifled and frustrated by being managed by inexperienced project managers as much as employers feared hiring people who simply did not know how to do the work. This employers' dilemma of available and inexpensive temps versus expensive but reliable permanent staff is well illustrated by a human resource director in an auto supplier interviewed by Erickcek and colleagues (2003: 381):

> As we were growing the business and ... trying to get product out the door, it's like, 'Get some more temporaries, get some more temporaries,' and one morning we woke up and we were at like 25 per cent. And ... quality is starting to have problems ... and now it's like, 'We've got to get this temporary ratio back down.' ... We'll start edging back down to 20, and ... then the goal becomes 15 per cent. We haven't hit it ... and now there's always this discussion, 'Well, it's more cost effective to have the temporaries.' So even though they talk about it, we are never going to get this high rate down. We run at around 20 per cent. So what I'm trying to say is, is there a cost advantage? If there is ... let's decide this and we're going to operate within 20 to 25 per cent. ... But ... we are in this constant state of denial, yet that number still stays up there and ... the vice president of human resources is ... [saying], 'We've got to get it down.'
>
> (Reproduced with permission of RUSSELL SAGE in the format 'Republish in a book' via Copyright Clearance Center.)

The significant aspect of these debates is the way that contingent contracts affect how people are managed. Employers use a wide range of practices to manage workers, from tight contractual control of work through trust, moral suasion, regulation, supervision, control, consent and commitment. Flexible contracts may limit the extent to which these can be used since employer and employee have less of a relationship, although as observed above, contractors may be trusted to possess and use their skills and 'repeat' temps are valued.

Redundancy

There is one final form of flexibility that is worth considering, and that is redundancy. Until the early 1990s, white collar office workers were often sheltered from the economic cycle and promised security of employment in exchange for loyalty. Their blue collar colleagues in the factories were less fortunate. Here, redundancy was a common occurrence, but it followed the economic cycle. When firms lost orders or the economy grew sluggish workers would be made redundant, when orders were won and the economy picked up they were often re-hired.

In the 1990s this changed as many employers realised that when they announced redundancies as part of a strategic restructuring their share prices rose. The salary bill was cut and work was generally intensified for the survivors, a strategy adopted even when the economy was buoyant (Cappelli, 1995). Van Wanrooy and colleagues (2013: 7) report 13 per cent of workplaces making compulsory redundancies and 7 per cent offering voluntary ones.

In the USA there are over 900,000 redundancies each year, compared to over 500,000 in the UK, and in China, between 1998 and 2001 more than 25 million workers were laid off from state-owned firms. It can be entertaining charting the various ways that HR departments euphemistically describe redundancy with expressions including payroll reduction, de-selection, downscoping, de-recruiting, slimming and career re-appraisal, but the reality is that redundancy is becoming a way of organising staff and reducing their numbers to an extent unmatched in the past (Redman et al., 2013) and in ways that can have devastating effects on the people made redundant. Ehrenreich's (2006) study, *Bait and Switch* charts the desperation of redundant professionals in the USA and their many (enthusiastic, pro-active, pop-psychology prompted) attempts to climb back on to the corporate ladder. These redundancies also have implications for corporate memory, controlling the way tasks are done and the way survivors view their employer. Small wonder then, that Tyler and Wilkinson (2007) call this process corporate anorexia, in which organisations constantly shed workers in pursuit of a corporate body that is more profitable and more desirable to shareholders.

Discussion and conclusions

So, given this dramatic increase in flexible and contingent work, does this mean that firms are starting to look like Atkinson's (1984) flexible firm with core and periphery workers employed in different ways? Not really. When Atkinson was writing a small number of large firms including

Proctor and Gamble in the USA and Unilever in the UK were experimenting with employing workers around a core and periphery, but there were never many of these.

The increase in flexibility has been caused, not primarily by large organisations strategically restructuring their employment relationships but by the growth of the service sector (for more on this see Chapter 7) and the fragmentation of large organisations and the public sector. Service sector work has long been characterised by atypical contracts. Many retail outlets and coffee bars are predominantly staffed by part-time workers, though managers are still expected to work full time. In the UK, large public sector employers are often required to put the services they provide out to tender, so that private employers can bid for, and run, individual parts of that service. For large private sector companies fragmentation may take the form of outsourcing, where goods are produced in places where wages are lower and services provided by external, specialist companies. According to the WERS survey 58 per cent of firms outsource their building maintenance, 48 per cent outsource cleaning, 35 per cent outsource training and 32 per cent outsource security (van Wanrooy et al., 2013: 43).

The extent of this fragmentation and the use of flexible contracts varies greatly from sector to sector. In some industries contingent working is a choice. A teacher can apply for a permanent job in a school or they may choose to register with a specialist agency to do 'supply' work (where they work as a temporary employee). The majority of the profession are employed on permanent contracts, either full- or part-time. In others, contingent contracts are the standard way of working. In film and TV production, outside the major terrestrial broadcasters, freelancers are hired project by project and most professionals are freelancers (Grugulis and Stoyanova, 2012).

In areas where high proportions of the workforce are employed on contingent contracts there are often worrying implications for skills. Firms which employ people part-time, through temporary employment agencies, on work outsourced by another organisation or only for a single project have far less incentive to train and develop them than those offering more secure employment (Grugulis and Vincent, 2005). Significantly, Barley and Kunda's (2004) contractors had all acquired high levels of skills while employed on traditional full-time contracts at the start of their careers. All were aware of the importance of maintaining and developing their skills and went to considerable lengths to ensure that they did so. In sectors where professionals may be freelance for their whole careers developing skills is much harder. Freelancers in TV production would often work for free, set up their own (unpaid) creative projects or borrow equipment to hone their skills, but, even with all this activity, they enjoyed far fewer learning opportunities than their predecessors who had been employed on permanent contracts by the major terrestrial broadcasters (Grugulis and Stoyanova, 2009). For those engaged in low-skilled work the problem is a little different since contingent contracts may cut them off from potential career ladders and opportunities for development, effectively restricting them to low-skilled, flexible contracts. Since flexibility is influenced by gender, race, class and nationality with women, migrant workers and those with few or no qualifications more likely to find themselves in numerically flexible, precarious work, this has worrying implications for equality.

For employers, flexibility offers short-term cost savings but these often come with long-term management problems. This 'low road' of numerical flexibility is often associated with lower rates of pay and fewer benefits. Firms which use it are *less* innovative than others. In other words, flexibility is increasing but not in the way that Atkinson predicted, where a mixture of different types of flexibility would be used strategically within a firm. Rather, it seems as though many firms are seizing the opportunity to pay workers less, employ them for fewer hours and give them less security.

Has this increase in flexible work had an impact on the extent to which the workplace is a market? Have people, as some commentators have argued, effectively commodified themselves, selling their work products readily, considering ways of marketing themselves more effectively and making rational decisions about their working time, space and duration? To a certain extent yes. Barley and Kunda's contractors devised attractive resumes, engaged in 'stretchwork' and sought out multiple agencies to make links to employers. However, as they also argue, work is not simply a commodity that can be bought and sold without concern, it is a social activity, a place where people form friendships and relationships, learn, counsel and mature. The reactions that their contractors and the permanent staff they worked with were not confined to rational purchase or sale decisions. Contractors noticed when they were made to share single cubicles in the least desirable part of the office, kept from having staff login codes or barred from staff perks like the use of bicycles to cycle round the work 'campus'. Whether on flexible contracts or not, workers still need to engage emotionally.

More prosaically, flexible work has financial implications for workers. For Barley and Kunda's contractors it meant higher rates of pay to compensate for the lack of stability and benefits. For other employees, it means a lack of both benefits and higher pay with which to purchase those benefits (such as pensions, insurance, holiday pay or redundancy cover) on the open market, or provide themselves with a savings 'cushion' to survive down times. What are the implications of this type of work for workers? Most significant is that a lack of security in employment (hours, contract) often results in a lack of security of income. Highly skilled workers still valued the freedom that working for themselves or being involved on a project-by-project basis could provide, but they earned enough to be able to save to cover fallow periods between projects and to save for retirement. For those lower down the pay scale who are shifted from 16 hours' work one week to 6 the next and 10 the week after, such fluctuations in pay are much harder to guard against since their pay is likely to be already too low to provide a buffer. These jobs outnumber the highly paid ones by a considerable margin. As Kalleberg (2013) observes in the USA, there has been a small growth in highly skilled, highly rewarded 'good' jobs and a substantial rise in precarious 'bad' jobs with little security and no access to health benefits or pensions.

Then there is the issue of who the employer actually is. A factory worker in China may work on outsourced Apple products, to Apple specifications but will receive their pay from, and be managed by Foxconn, their employer. An agency worker is legally the employee of the agency, and will be paid by that agency but they are likely to work on client premises and act under orders from client supervisors. For some employers this is a way of avoiding responsibilities, of distancing themselves from oppressive supervision, low rates of pay and poor records of health and safety.

Thompson and McHugh (2002: 179) call this increase in flexibility a 'somewhat one-sided bargain'. Workers are asked to give more of themselves, in exchange for which employers give less. A small number of highly skilled professionals have gained, both financially and in terms of control over their working lives, but the majority of those employed on flexible contracts are not highly skilled IT workers and do not enjoy their advantages.

6

Employee Voice

A key aspect of human resource management is the voice employees have at work. This can take a variety of forms and different schemes may harness employees' expertise on the production line to spot faults, keep quality levels high or cover for team-mates. Alternatively, employees may be part of organisational decision making, through formal works councils and worker directors sitting permanently on the company board or by being consulted about major decisions on an *ad hoc* basis.

The idea behind all of these initiatives is that workplaces are improved, that productivity levels are higher and that workers are more satisfied when they have a voice in work processes. Much of this makes sense. It is the workers on the factory line in manufacturing companies who know most about what happens in their area so it is good practice to harness that expertise. Those on the front-desk in customer service roles are the principal point of contact for customers. If they can resolve problems themselves, without passing a query or complaint on to other workers, customer satisfaction is likely to be higher. When a firm is planning significant changes such as relocation or redundancies, they need to manage the changes without alienating their remaining workers. There is already a well-known problem called 'survivor syndrome' in which even those employees not selected for redundancy feel alienated, disengaged and insecure. At each of these levels practice is improved and consent is more easily won when employees have a voice in the process. The strength of that voice, as well as the form that it takes, is likely to vary. Employees may be *consulted* by managers. When this happens they are told what is happening and asked for their views, but have no power to influence the final decision. Alternatively, workers may be *involved* in the decision making; managers still retain the ultimate decision-making power but employees have input into the process. Finally, employees may *participate* in the decision making and joint groups of employees and managers may meet to discuss issues and make key decisions.

Voice is heard in all (and occasionally none) of these ways in organisations and in this chapter we will consider the involvement, participation and empowerment of employees. We will consider the successes of different schemes and also the various problems, failures and (often predictable) difficulties each face, together with the varying degrees of efficiency and effectiveness with which schemes are managed and the effect they have on employees.

The chapter starts by distinguishing between involvement and participation and examines the extent and depth of various schemes. It considers empowerment and trust within these two areas. At every stage we question the amount of power devolved to employees. Judged by their own rhetoric, these schemes result in a substantial shift of power. Judged by workplace realities, not much changes. Some adjustments may be made and work may be intensified but it is difficult to argue that any form of employee voice marks a dramatic shift in worker power and leads to workplace democracies. Voice is often confined to trivial tasks or issues, with little real power. This may not matter. Employee voice schemes can work extremely well and, even when they grant workers very limited levels of discretion, they are still appreciated when they are introduced in workplaces with very low levels of trust. As Geary (2003: 338) says, employee participation is 'still limited, still controlled, but still welcome'.

Participation and involvement

Participation and involvement can take a variety of forms. Wilkinson et al.'s (2013) escalator of involvement illustrates this well. On the bottom step we have *information*, then comes *communication*, where employees are allowed to respond with their own views, *consultation*, when those views may be taken into account, *co-determination* when decisions are taken jointly by both employees and managers and finally *control* where the company itself is controlled by the workers.

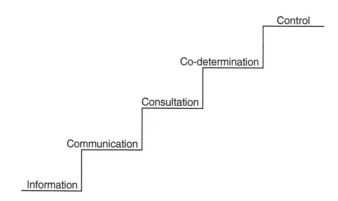

Figure 6.1 The escalator of participation

Source: Managing human resources: human resource management in transition by Bach, S. and Edwards, M.R. (2013, p.270). Reproduced with permission of Wiley in the format 'Book' via Copyright Clearance Center.

So, information might take the form of company newsletters, magazines, e-mails, regularly updated noticeboards, websites or announcements by supervisors. These can be useful mechanisms for letting employees know what is going on in the rest of the organisation, for publicising social events, celebrating achievements or issuing reminders.

Communication goes a little further, since through it employees may have opportunities to feed their views back to management, as well as listening to the messages that management provide. Shop-floor meetings may be focused on official presentations but can also provide space for questions and feedback; managers and supervisors may deal with employees individually or collectively; while suggestion boxes and company surveys allow for written feedback. Thirdly comes consultation. In this, workers can speak and are consulted over aspects of work. This might include Staff Councils, with employee representatives, consultations for a specific project such as redundancies or relocation or discussions with union representatives. Managers have the final decision, but workers are involved in that decision-making process.

Then comes co-determination where decisions are taken jointly. It is likely to involve the same institutional structures as consultation, with staff councils and employee representatives, but, rather than employee views being reported back to management, who take the final decision, with co-determination the decision-making process is shared. Finally comes control, in which it is workers who run the company. Co-operatives are one example of this. In them employees own as well as work in the organisation, and decisions are taken jointly. Most co-operatives are small firms, facilitating personal contact between worker-owners but some, such as the John Lewis Partnership, are large and successful.

This 'escalator of involvement' is a useful model because it differentiates clearly between various types of involvement and participation, showing their depth (or shallowness) and the type of activity that each comprises. But it is also misleading. When we see an escalator or a stairway it implies some kind of progression (either up or down). Here there is no such dynamism. Firms that have highly successful newsletters may have no reason to progress to staff surveys, works councils or joint negotiating committees. Those which consult over compulsory redundancies will not necessarily institutionalise the process so that employees have a voice over other issues that impact on them. Each step on the escalator indicates a different level of involvement, but the escalator itself is not moving.

Nor are these steps of equal size. The most common forms of involvement are the ones in which workers have the least voice, such as information and communication. Indeed, the lowest step on the escalator, *information,* gives workers no voice at all. Many firms have newsletters, but far fewer allow opportunities for employees to respond. According to *People Management* magazine, the figures for information and communication are quite impressive with 80 per cent of firms communicating with their employees through team meetings and line manager one-to-one discussions and 74 per cent using staff surveys (Stevens, 2012). Set against this, only 13 per cent of companies have Joint Consultative Committees (van Wanrooy et al., 2013). Co-operatives are extremely rare and there is little evidence that their numbers are increasing.

It is also important to consider *what* employees are involved in, or consulted over. Managers may be happy to delegate organising the Christmas party, redecorating the staff common room or deciding what food should be served in the canteen; but employees are likely to be granted considerably less responsibility and discretion over their organisation's five-year strategy and consultations over departmental changes may not necessarily lead to involvement in wider organisational issues. Nissan's problem-solving meetings are described below and these give teams of workers considerable discretion over specific aspects of the manufacturing process, but, as Blyton and Turnbull (1998) point out, they control little else.

Employee involvement

Since the 1980s, most of the schemes through which workers have gained a voice at work can be classified as *employee involvement.* These tend to be initiated by management, task based and involve limited levels of discretion around one particular activity. Nissan's teams are a good example of this. Blyton and Turnbull (1998) draw on Popham (1992) to describe the way short team meetings at the start of every shift prompt the workers to address day-to-day problems (1998: 217):

> The supervisor and the twenty men (compromising two teams, each with a team leader) leave the meeting room where they have been chatting and reading newspapers prior to the shift commencing, and go out onto the shop-floor. They congregate in a circle round the presses while the supervisor discusses a problem they had encountered the previous day with some faulty pressings, which had got through as far as the paint shop. The upshot of this discussion is that one of the group is detailed to go down to the paint shop and go through the stack of parts waiting to be painted, in order to find the faulty ones (Popham, 1992).

Such five-minute meetings, run across the Nissan factory in Sunderland, also deal with work schedule changes, work redistribution, process changes, training, social events or introducing new members of the team, because one of Nissan's principles is to delegate responsibility to the shop-floor. Meetings are short, practical and can resolve problems quickly and inexpensively (in this instance, the problem was spotted and solved before the cars had left the factory).

Allowing front-line staff to make decisions can be extremely success-ful. Batt's (2004) study of team-working in the telecommunications industry in the USA revealed that not only could workers take on internal co-ordination effectively, organising assignments and arrang-ing quality inspections and safety reports; they also liaised with other departments and external companies.

So, involvement can be a means of ensuring that tasks are completed more efficiently. Problems can be spotted earlier and resolved at a local level, tasks can be organised effectively and personal preferences given appropriate consideration. More cynically, they can also be a way for organisations to intensify work, tapping into workers' discretionary efforts and harnessing their expertise as well as their hands, generally for few additional rewards. Batt's (2004) telecommunications workers reported significantly higher levels of satisfaction but no increases in pay.

As well as being a method for completing tasks effectively, employee involvement can also be a marketing device for management; a means of winning workers' consent for changes that have already been planned. Royal Mail introduced an experimental scheme in which machine operators undertook additional training, assumed responsibility for the basic maintenance and cleaning of their machine and were encouraged to suggest improvements to the workplace and work processes. It proved a fruitful exercise and, at first glance, appeared to be task focused (Noon et al., 2000: 508–509):

Team leader:	What changes have been made as a result of [the team-working and involvement initiative] then?
Operator D:	We've changed the layout of [names machine] work area to a U-shape [physical layout].
Team leader:	Has it affected the throughputs?
Operator E:	It's a lot quicker to see the jams.
Operator C:	There's better vision now.
Engineer:	There's better access now.
Team leader:	What other changes have you made?

Operator B: We've put a light in the culler section.

Operator E: A new belt on the in-feeder.

Operator A: We've fitted a reverse paddle.

Operator D: There's a new stamping table, there is the wheels and a new part of the table.

Team leader: You see these ideas have come about through the management and the team – it's not rocket science!

[Encouraged by this, they list five other changes]

When the researchers probed a little further it appeared that part of that success was artificial. Several workers commented that changes, including the introduction of the U-shaped working area, had actually been suggested by management. Pateman (1970) refers to this as *pseudo-participation*, activities which are essentially management persuasion initiatives. So, involvement can see workers with increased voice at task level. Some firms, such as Nissan, give teams the authority to organise work, set rotas and resolve basic problems. In others, such as Royal Mail, major changes are planned by management, but discussed and agreed by the team of workers, who may also have ideas on how these plans are implemented.

Empowerment

These examples raise questions over the extent to which involved employees exercise any real power. Organisations often stress the importance of employees' influence, saying that these involvement and team-working activities *empower* employees with staff given responsibility and expected to police themselves. Companies can eliminate layers of management, employees will be psychologically healthier, work more interesting and less alienating.

All of this sounds entirely positive. However, as with most other HR practices, we need to be cautious. There may well be a difference between the advantages promised and the results that individuals and organisations experience. There is certainly a sharp distinction between the way the word empowerment has been traditionally used and the management practices it has come to describe. The idea of empowerment comes from feminist and social movement writers (Fenton-O' Creevy, 1995: 154 cited in Edwards and Collinson, 2002: 273). Empowerment used to mean providing individuals (usually disadvantaged) with the tools and resources to further their own interests, *as they see them*. Within the field of management, empowerment is commonly used with a different meaning: providing employees with tools, resources and discretion to further the interests of the organisation (as seen by senior management).

Despite this narrowing of the term's remit, there is still room for genuine increases in workers' discretion over the work that they do. Edwards and Collinson (2002: 277) suggest that, for this to be achieved, employees should be given broad objectives rather than a pre-defined task, as well as the right to access the means to achieve these objectives (resources, training), authority to make decisions on their own initiative and the right to debate and challenge the goals that are set.

There are instances of significant levels of responsibility being devolved in this way. One example of this was an Alcan aluminium smelter in Canada, described by Belanger and colleagues (2003). Management and the union together designed a system of self-managing teams which controlled 10 key tasks including calling co-workers for overtime, calling team meetings, co-ordination between production and maintenance, and following up repairs to ensure these complied with health and safety. There were only 24 supervisors for 444 workers and neither supervisors nor managers worked at night or weekends (although one supervisor was on call and could be paged at home if necessary). Workers said this absence of supervision was not a problem, 'We know what needs to be done!' (2003: 242).

When it came to the day-to-day running of the factory, workers were empowered to make the routine decisions and did so, with few problems. But the conditions here were unusual. Smelters are long-term investments which cannot easily be moved, so job security was good and the workforce was fully unionised. Teams had been designed collaboratively by management and unions. There was a high level of trust and an impressive proportion of long-serving staff with 86 per cent of employees having worked at Alcan for more than 20 years.

Other examples of empowerment are less impressive. McDonald's claimed to have empowered customer service staff when it allowed them to use their own discretion over which greeting to use, instead of insisting on the much mocked 'have a nice day'. Tupperware empowered its party sales staff, according to one enthusiastic dealer by giving them the freedom to choose which colour plastic containers to display:

> The company gives me great freedom to develop my own approach. There are certain elements that need to be in every party to make it successful, but if those elements are coloured by you, a Tupperware

dealer – purple, pink and polka dot, and I prefer it lavender and lace –
that's okay. That freedom allows you to be the best that you are capable
of being. (Peters and Waterman, 1982; Willmott, 1993: 526)

The choice between purple, pink and polka dot, and lavender and lace
is a trivial one. Unfortunately, there seem to be many more empowerment schemes granting discretion over trivialities than offering
substantive responsibility. Worse, Hales' (2000) research observes
empowerment associated with low staffing levels, responsibility for
satisfying customers (often without the resources to make this achievable) and reductions in the numbers and role of junior managers. In
other words, workers are set up to fail and take the blame, and all in
the name of empowerment.

Realistically most forms of involvement are extremely limited. Firms
use the buzz words, but what is done is not particularly dramatic.
Team-working has been a widely used HR practice for some years.
Evidence from studies such as Batt's (2004) showed clearly that it had
an effect, that workers in teams could manage themselves and take
responsibility for a wide range of tasks and that this was not only a
more efficient way of working – it was also more satisfying for the
workers. Hardly surprising then, that 65 per cent of organisations
reported implementing team-working with their largest occupational
group. However, few were the type of self-managed teams in Batt's
study. In all, 62 per cent of companies reported that these individuals
worked with each other, 54 per cent that they had responsibility for a
specific product or service, 35 per cent that they decided how work was
to be done and a mere 3 per cent that they appointed their own team
leaders (Cully et al., 1999).

When involvement fails

Most management textbooks concentrate on reporting successes. This is
understandable. Managers are interested in triumphs, rather than disasters; firms only want to publicise initiatives when they get them right; and
successes make a pretty good story. Unfortunately what this can mean is
that the majority of HR initiatives, which don't work, simply get swept
under the carpet. Here, by contrast, we are going to look at some unsuc-
cessful initiatives and consider *why* each failed. We can, after all, learn as
much (if not more) from disasters as from triumphs and since problem
cases easily outnumber successes it is probably more important to focus
on them. Each, also, tells us a great deal about the way organisations
work. These failures include problems communicating, a badly designed

initiative (revealed by a badly designed kettle), bad timing and simple failures to extend successful trials.

Our first example is 'Britarm', a large retail bank which formally set aside 30 minutes every Wednesday morning for communication meetings to allow branches, departments and offices to listen to organisational news, share problems and bond with colleagues (Weeks, 2004). However, having scheduled this unstructured time, senior executives worried that it might be wasted and developed detailed briefings, scripts and videos designed to fill the meetings, effectively subverting the original purpose of the time, which was to allow staff to communicate with each other. Local managers, who frequently cancelled meetings, were generally grateful for the guidance, since it relieved them of the obligation of leading the meetings. Ironically this head office material did ensure that the meetings became bonding experiences, though not quite in the way anticipated. Staff and managers united in mockery and criticism of the scripts, dress sense, mannerisms and management speak they were presented with. One manager, when questioned on part of his script, simply rolled his eyes and replied, '[y]ou know the Bank' (2004: 18).

If simple communications meetings can go wrong, more thorough attempts at involving employees are even more risky. When Phillips introduced employee involvement, shop-floor workers used a feedback meeting to raise concerns about a flaw in one of the kettles the company made. The design of the kettle's handle made it harder to assemble, with the result that the workers could not meet production or quality targets. Since their bonuses depended on reaching these targets, that particular design fault was a major problem. At the meeting managers claimed that they had not known about this fault. Two weeks later, when they had still done nothing to address it, the head of the design department admitted that tight schedules and limited staffing meant that problems could only be dealt with during a set testing period before production started. After that, there was no opportunity to fix any flaws. Phillips had not told the workers this when setting up the involvement scheme, nor did the managers reveal it when the workers repeatedly challenged the design flaw that prevented them reaching their targets.

Less impressively, Lewisham Council 'empowered' some of its customer service staff at the same time as cutting their pay, benefits, sickness pay and holiday leave. Unsurprisingly morale sank to 'rock bottom' (Edwards and Collinson, 2002).

Lastly come two slightly different 'failures'; these were two successful involvement schemes which were never extended beyond their original trial group and remained peripheral. The Royal Mail scheme which generated so many positive suggestions was an experimental initiative, confined to a single machine. When the newly trained operatives, now accustomed to take responsibility for their machines, were sent to work elsewhere they had to return to standard ways of working, even if this meant ignoring minor problems until they became major ones. One operative commented that (Noon et al., 2000: 510):

> Last week I was working on the pre-sorter and it was playing up. I told the gaffer the machine wasn't working and that I knew what was going wrong but didn't know why. I thought to myself, I'm doing preventative maintenance here, but my gaffer wasn't interested, he said, wait until it has broken down. So the engineer came after it had broken down.

In Batt's research, even though the teams could manage themselves very successfully, they were not always allowed to do so (2004: 203):

> In general we've gotten support from upper management, but the supervisors won't let go. The supervisor still makes the decisions and we do the paperwork. We're not invited in on decisions made by the supervisor. She decides overtime; we can't set our work schedule. So she basically treats the traditional and self-directed groups the same.

When questioned, senior management confirmed that they were unlikely to extend the scheme, since it was not popular with supervisors, who felt, quite rightly, that they were losing power as a result.

There are a number of issues here. Communication is not effectively introduced, involvement schemes are designed to elicit contributions only during a (narrow) window and employees are not informed of this, schemes designed to encourage positive behaviours are swamped by negative actions and, even when successful, schemes are not extended because they threaten the existing power structures. Set against their own criteria for success – communicating with staff, increasing motivation and increasing efficiency – these schemes have not been successful and most of the failures are entirely predictable. Everything that an organisation does sends messages to its staff, and workers are not slow to spot contradictions. The videos of head office managers at Britarm bank giving messages that clashed with employees' daily experience of what Britarm was like as an employer were simply greeted with mockery and cheerful cynicism. Not a disaster, but certainly not a success, nor the reaction the senior management hoped to inspire.

The Phillips scheme is interesting because it, like the unfortunate kettle, was not well designed. Workers were encouraged to suggest changes, but, for these to be put into practice, they needed to be made during the first few weeks of the development cycle. Management had not told workers this and did not tell them even when management's failure to act meant that the workers would lose their bonus. The original reluctance to tell workers about the limited window for change may have been a form of pseudo-participation, intended to encourage greater emotional engagement, with workers encouraged to contribute because it stimulated them to think about their work and put additional effort in. Management's failure to reveal the truth, or take another form of action (such as changing the production targets) even when bonuses depended on it was likely to turn a motivational scheme into a disaster, when workers realised they had been tricked into suggesting improvements which would never be made.

While Phillips' scheme was potentially successful and became a disaster only through (deliberately) poor communication and misguided attempts to conceal problems from the workforce, Lewisham's began and ended as a disaster. Whatever the merits of the empowerment scheme itself, it was not good tactics to introduce it while other terms and conditions were being slashed.

Even when schemes are successful, as in Royal Mail (Noon et al., 2000) or the telecommunications company studied by Batt (2004), successful pilots may not always be extended since team-working and giving workers' discretion can challenge existing power relations or ways of doing work. This may generate concerns. The supervisors in Batt's study certainly worried about whether such a delegation of responsibility was intended to eliminate the need for supervisors. In fact there was no such hidden agenda and they were reassured but other organisations have used team-working to restructure and make redundancies so these concerns were legitimate.

Employee participation

While employee involvement is initiated by management, largely task focused and limited in scope, participation has the potential to be a little broader. Through it, workers *participate* in decisions at a variety of levels in firms. These decisions may include issues around corporate governance, management, staff pay and benefits, relocations and redundancies. For the pluralists (who take workplace conflict to be natural and inevitable, but see the job of management and unions as managing this through institutions, systems and procedures, see Chapter 1), such participation is vital in order for organisations to function, with works councils and Joint Consultative Committees (JCCs) serving as spaces where all the different interests can meet to discuss their difficulties and agree constructive routes forward.

This, at least, is the theory. One particularly long-standing example of partnership in practice is that of Tesco's, a major supermarket, and USDAW, the Union of Shop, Distributive and Allied Workers. The official partnership, *Working Better Together* was established in 1998. It involves a series of staff forums in which management, union representatives and employee representatives meet several times a year. Forums take place at store (three grouped stores for the very small Tesco Express outlets), regional and national levels. They discuss performance, ways of working, corporate issues, and employees' terms and conditions. Individual staff members can raise issues and both they, and their trade union representatives, have access to the highest levels of management (Blyton and Turnbull, 2004).

At one level this is very positive. Staff can participate in decision making on a whole range of issues, including pay. Representatives have direct access to senior management and senior management have direct access to front line staff. Management still have the final say, but the structural features of the partnership ensure that staff are consulted regularly over a whole range of concerns. However, as Blyton and Turnbull (2004), observe, most managers acknowledge that workers are *not* involved in decisions on matters that affect their jobs. In other words, while there is a great deal of consultation, there is little transfer of power. Management make and take the decisions, the partnership structures assist in communications.

Traditionally, of course, workers participated indirectly in decision making via their trade unions. Employers and unions would negotiate with one another (a process called collective bargaining) (Heery, 2014). Workers gained strength by acting together and union power stemmed from the number of people they represented, as well as their capacity to take action. This participation extended considerably beyond that offered by Tesco's in its partnership deal. Indeed, historically, it has been unions which have secured the eight hour day, weekends, increased holidays and better terms and conditions for workers. Ramsay (1977) argued that all forms of participation are cyclical and the result of workers' power, rather than management's generosity. Workers always want a voice at work, but that demand is only met when they are comparatively powerful. So, during the First World War, when conscription reduced the labour force just as wartime production stimulated demand for goods, workplace councils were established. These lost influence later, when unemployment rose and workers' power waned.

In the present day, few workplaces have formal systems of participation that centre on trade union representation. A major reason for this is that UK union membership, having peaked at more than 13 million in 1979, has been in decline for some years and stood at 6.4 million in

2014 (DBIS, 2015: 5). Unions still represent individual members and, in the public sector the union voice is strong, with 57 per cent of public sector workers trade union members. In most of the private sector that voice is a whisper – 14 per cent of private sector workers belong to trade unions (Johnstone, 2014: 153) and only 4 per cent of private sector workplaces still set employees' pay by collective bargaining (van Wanrooy et al., 2013: 80).

The form of participation and partnership offered to unions by employers such as Tesco's is very different to the voice many unions have traditionally achieved through collective bargaining and direct action. This is often a source of dissent within the unions with critics arguing that these arrangements may make unions focus on pleasing management, to keep partnerships stable, rather than challenging problems or campaigning for members' rights. In one company in Ireland, where management and unions had agreed to a 'no strike' deal and where the partnership forum, which should have represented employees, rarely met, workers' frustration was expressed through increased absenteeism and the formation of not one, but two, new and more radical unions (Dundon and Dobbins, 2015). Elsewhere, conflict and consensus co-exist within fairly successful partnerships. Cook and colleagues (forthcoming) document management boasting about using the union to simply pass messages on; while the union, in return, conveniently 'forgot' to inform members of messages they disagreed with. Far from aiming to placate management, this union was still able to challenge it over health and safety as well as problems with training.

In other countries, where systems of industrial relations are different, participation is both widespread and widely used. In Germany, the Netherlands and France there are long standing traditions that management and unions negotiate over a wide range of issues, including training and work design. JCCs allow managers and employee representatives to meet and there are worker representatives on company boards. In 2005 the Information and Consultation of Employees (ICE) Regulations were passed, intended to encourage the spread of such practices around the EU. They have had little effect on the UK. In firms employing over 100 workers the number of JCCs has increased, but overall the proportion of companies with a JCC declined from 9 per cent in 2004 to 8 per cent in 2011; for companies with more than 50 employees this decline was from 14 per cent to 13 per cent (van Wanrooy et al., 2013: 61).

Even outside these regulations unions can have a significant influence on employee voice. McBride (2008) describes the way that the Tyneside unions organised regular 'grouse' meetings, providing a forum where problems could be aired, discussed, challenged and resolved. In the past,

UK trade unions have been powerful representatives for employee voice and in some workplaces today this still holds true, but declining union membership means that, outside the public sector, that voice is muted and the partnership arrangements offered by employers have been more limited in scope and influence. Financial participation, which some commentators claimed might fill the breach via a shareholder democracy rather than a trade union democracy, is better at providing bonuses than voice. There are numerous employee share ownership programmes, particularly in the USA and Japan, but the rewards tend to be heavily skewed towards senior management. Most employees have little power to improve the value of their holdings but can suffer when these go down. Top management can and do benefit from being awarded very high numbers of shares, but it is not clear whether this aligns their interests with the firm or simply increases their potential rewards.

In principle shareholder meetings can provide another opportunity for voice since formal presentations are made about the business and shareholders have the opportunity to vote on a small number of issues but for most large firms few shareholders use these meetings as an opportunity to exercise decision making and groups of employees are likely to hold too few shares to make much of an impact.

Partnership has had a number of well-publicised successes. It helps to underpin co-operative and trust-based industrial relations in Germany. Yet outside a small number of countries it exists in only a minority of firms and there to a limited extent.

Trust

A key aspect of the partnership process is trust; if neither side trusts the other then the success of any partnership programme is likely to be limited. Most employees say their managers are not in favour of unions (van Wanrooy et al., 2013) and, as Kelly (1996: 88) points out, 'it is difficult, if not impossible to have a partnership with a party who would prefer you didn't exist'. Yet, it is possible for partnership to make some inroads, even in conditions of low trust and historical hostility. Dietz's (2004) study of Allied Distillers had most employees forthrightly reporting 'no trust whatsoever'. Unsurprisingly, a number of attempts to achieve partnership failed, implementation was inept and both sides were unwilling to share materials with the other. The breakthrough came when, following repeated failed attempts at establishing a partnership, management started sharing genuinely confidential information. Workers, guaranteed that there would be 'no losers' and they would have job security, introduced new, flexible working practices. Everyone's pay went up.

Impressive as these achievements were, given the legacy of conflict, they did not prove to be long lasting. After three years some of the key players who had negotiated the partnership agreement left the company, management started to encroach on some of the prerogatives they had granted to the workers (including the right to set their own break times) and problems arose. The partnership did continue, but it was extremely shaky.

Discussion and conclusions

There are a number of key lessons here. Employee voice can take a wide variety of forms, depths and responsibilities. Participation sees decisions shared as of right. It is rooted in ideas of social justice and democracy and, through it, workers are an integral part of organisational decision making. Involvement, by contrast, is task-based and initiated by management. Parts may be influenced by the Human Relations school of management thought, which seeks to secure employee commitment from good communication and decent treatment at work. But its primary aim is efficiency, with responsibility devolved because this is a sensible way to organise work. Schemes are different, but it would be misleading to assume that they are primarily initiated to humanise working conditions. They are not. Their focus is generally workplace efficiency, something the HR rhetoric surrounding them may conceal.

Understanding and appreciating this diversity is important. After all, if we are assessing whether a particular scheme has worked, part of that will involve asking exactly *what* a scheme has been successful at. Launching a company newsletter, for example, may mean that a firm successfully informs staff about a range of topics but, of itself, it is unlikely to impact engagement or productivity.

Unfortunately, when assessed against their own rhetoric most schemes fail and not simply because, as in the examples above, they are introduced at hopelessly inappropriate times, are poorly designed, never progress beyond the pilot stage or suffer from other practical problems with implementation. Rather, when assessed against their own rhetoric most schemes fail because that rhetoric is an unsuitable measure. Indeed, claiming incongruous accomplishments in advance seems to be a feature of many HR practices.

Some academic authors have used this rhetoric to argue that these schemes have totalitarian tendencies, and it is certainly true that the language used points in that direction. In reality however, workers are not cultural dupes and are more than capable of judging their employers' actions, of participating in schemes because it is their job, because they seek praise or promotion, or because they gain pleasure from them (as well as avoiding participation where necessary). It is not helpful to develop an extreme model of empowerment and then say organisations do not achieve it. Managers and workers both tend to have mundane objectives.

Employee involvement often does result in work intensification, or in expanding job responsibilities with workers expected to think about their work, offer suggestions on ways in which it could be improved, or taking charge of particular aspects of work. Developments which may be welcomed or resisted by the workers themselves. In understanding these responses the context of each intervention is particularly important, since the way initiatives are received is likely to depend very heavily on workers' previous experiences (Edwards and Collinson, 2002).

Using this reality check also helps us to assess the worth of schemes. Most employee voice initiatives simply do not confer significant amounts of decision-making power on employees, nor do they empower them to make decisions, challenge existing hierarchies or assume responsibilities. With some notable exceptions, the power they devolve, the work activities and the decision making are all relatively trivial. Few employees can challenge the strategic direction of their firms, or the way production is organised. That said, simply because they do not confer substantial amounts of power, does not mean that they are worthless. As Edwards and Collinson (2002) note, most workers do not want to control the companies they work for. Involvement and participation schemes may give employees a small amount of voice over issues that affect them, information and communication initiatives will provide them with news about the company. It is not a particularly big deal, but it is much nicer than not being told.

7

Service Work

One of the most remarkable changes to the world of work over the last half century has been the growth in service sector employment. Today, in every developed country in the world, as well as in almost all of the developing world, the majority of the working population are employed in the service sector. In the UK 79 per cent of people in employment work in the service sector (ONS, 2015a). This is an amazing shift, and one that earlier generations of economists would not have considered possible. Indeed Adam Smith (1776/1993), in his classical text, *The Wealth of Nations* believed that services was where money was spent, rather than earned. This is a rather one-sided view. To the manufacturing worker the service sector may indeed be the place where they spend some of their earnings: eating lunch in a café, buying tickets to the theatre, paying for repairs to their car, or downloading a new game to their computers. However, in spending this money, our manufacturing worker is adding to the profits of cafés, theatres, garages and computer games companies; as well as keeping barristas, waiting staff, café managers, actors, writers, directors, producers, box office workers, set builders, props specialists, front and back of house staff, games designers, programmers, animators and artists in employment. The service sector is large, it can be profitable (both for individual firms and for the economy as a whole), and it is worthy of study.

This chapter starts by trying to define what service work is and reviewing some of the reasons for the shift from manufacturing to services before going on to look at one particular type of service sector worker in detail; the front line service worker, involved in 'high touch' (McDowell, 2009) work. It examines emotional and aesthetic labour, the way service sector workers are required to use their emotions and appearance as part of their job, and the impact that the customer has on the work process. Many service workers are very satisfied with their jobs, particularly the customer facing aspects, since sorting out people's problems and dealing with pleasant customers can be a source of considerable pleasure. However, not all customers are pleasant and much service work is poorly paid and tightly regulated so we will also be exploring the development of the emotional proletariat

(Hochschild, 1983), the ways that service sector workers can and do fight back and some of the problems they experience.

What is service work?

There have been many attempts to provide definitions of service sector work. Marek Korczynski (2002) considers five properties that service work may have: intangibility, perishability, variability, simultaneous production and consumption and inseparability. Other sectors make, manufacture or mine objects that you can drop on your foot. Service work does not and is *intangible*. Service sector goods and services are *perishable*: a seat on a particular flight cannot be kept in a storeroom until it is needed, once the flight has taken off it is no longer possible to book a passenger onto it, it can no longer be sold. Much service work involves dealing with customers so it is *variable*; one waiter may provide a very different standard of service to that offered by their colleagues, in terms of interaction with customers, familiarity with their preferences or level of engagement. Since it is a service that is being sold, activities are *produced* by workers *at the same moment* that they are *consumed* by customers. Finally, in the service sector, the customer is an *inseparable* part of what is being sold. It is the customers in a restaurant who initiate the orders for food and drink. The times at which they arrive and leave may be difficult to predict. They may personalise their order by asking for their food to be cooked in a particular way or requesting that side dishes be added and foods they are not fond of be left out. Without the customer, there would be no service process.

These five elements are useful, but they are not a perfect definition of services, nor does every service sector occupation involve all of these five features. When actors make a film there is a clear gap between the movie's production and its consumption by fans; retailing generally involves the exchange of tangible products as well as the process of being served; repairing a car requires physical changes to various component parts, and a pharmacist may prepare medication before it is ordered to provide a buffer for busy periods of the day. All are still classified as service sector work.

Service sector jobs are diverse, in part because the service sector is not a distinctive area of the economy, but a fairly messy agglomeration of 'everything else'. It covers shipping, railways, road and air transport, telecommunications, wholesale and retail distribution, and defence as well as hospitality, tourism and maintenance and repair. It is a pretty heterogeneous grouping in which firms seem to be defined by what they do *not* do, rather than what they do. These are firms that are *not* engaged in agriculture, that do *not* extract or refine natural resources, that do *not* build houses, and that do *not* manufacture products. Apart from that, they have little in common.

The sector encompasses a wide variety of industries with an even wider range of occupations. Many of these occupations are very similar to those in traditional manufacturing. Engineers repair aeroplanes, trains and lorries; logistics experts plan and adjust routes; warehouse workers package and stack deliveries. Here, in terms of worker skills and the nature of the work being performed, there is very little difference between someone who manufactures a motorbike and someone who repairs it (Grugulis, 2014). In this chapter our focus is not on these jobs, but on high touch customer facing work. This wider view of the sector as a whole serves to give a sense of the scale and context, after all, not all service sector occupations involve the aspects of work we consider here, just as not all service sector occupations involve knowledge work, or creativity or innovation.

So, what is high touch customer facing work and in what way(s) is it a distinctive form of employment? In this chapter we will look at three aspects of high touch customer facing work. The first is the way that workers' emotions, the way they feel and the feelings they provoke in others, have become part of work. The second – relatedly – is the way that an employee's appearance has become part of work, and the third is the role the customer plays.

Clearly these aspects of work are not confined to the high touch areas of the service sector. The emphasis on team-working in manufacturing has brought with it an interest in soft skills and emotions on the factory floor. That given, it is often the service sector where the management of emotions and aesthetics can be seen most vividly, so studying them here should help to clarify what such work involves and what the implications of it are, for both employees and employers.

The growth of the service sector

So, to take a step back, why is it that the service sector has grown so much in recent years? And, a related question, why are so many fewer people working in manufacturing? In June 2015 just over 3 million people were working in the manufacturing sector, about 10 per cent of those in employment (ONS, 2015a), yet some 60 years before, halfway through the twentieth century, this sector employed more than half of all workers (McDowell, 2009: 2). This shift to services has been mirrored in many other countries. In the USA, by the 1990s, more people were employed by McDonald's than by US Steel (Macdonald and Sirianni, 1996a). In the 1950s and 1960s we thought of work as an activity performed full time, by men in factories. By the twenty-first century people were far more likely to hold jobs in shops, cafés or call centres than in manufacturing industry.

Part of the reason for this is that much work has been automated. Car manufacturers have machinery that welds parts together, replacing skilled welders and some factories even use a process called *lights out manufacturing* in which all (or almost all) of the production process is automated. It is hardly surprising then, that while manufacturing still contributes significantly to national earnings (GDP) it employs far fewer people than it did 40 years ago. In addition to this, in many countries, outsourcing, specialist agencies and fragmenting organisations have resulted in some reclassification of jobs between sectors. The payroll department of a manufacturing firm would be classified as manufacturing, because the staff working there were the employees of a manufacturing company. If the manufacturing firm outsourced its payroll function to a specialist HR company those same payroll staff, doing the same work and organising the same payrolls, would be reclassified as service sector workers.

Automation can be an attractive option for companies. It may involve a substantial investment in plant and machinery, but if this means that fewer people need to be employed, the overall savings can be substantial, as can the impact on predictability and reliability. Taken together, these factors account for much of the decline in manufacturing employment. Work has been automated and outsourced, specialist services reclassified and firms reorganised.

'High touch' service sector work

Service sector work has not been immune from this process of automation. Vending machines sell crisps, sweets, coffees and hot chocolate drinks and in Royal Mail sorting offices, mail is organised by automatic sorting machines which scan the postcodes on the envelopes and arrange them accordingly. The service sector also has an additional resource, their customers, who can be co-opted into the service process and persuaded to perform tasks previously done for them. In fast food outlets customers place orders themselves on screen at quick pay points; airline passengers can book tickets and check in luggage online before flying; supermarket shoppers load their own trolleys and baskets, and increasingly scan the goods, pack them into bags and pay without assistance from cashiers or checkout staff, a marked contrast to the old corner shop where the shop-keeper would select, pack and often deliver groceries.

Successful as these initiatives are in reducing the amount of paid labour necessary to complete tasks, not all work is suitable for automation, delegation to customers or outsourcing. High touch and caring roles in particular rely on the presence of a worker. Parents who want their children collected at the end of the school day cannot really outsource this to China or India, nor can they send a machine to do the job. An elderly person who needs support to live independently relies on people for this and few hairdressers would use a robot to assess or cut hair. Such high touch, caring roles require people to do them.

Many high touch service sector workers are familiar features of our everyday lives: the barrista who prepares our lattes; the call centre customer service representative who answers queries about our bank account and the shop assistant who hands over change for our purchases. Observing them, academics from human resource management and industrial relations traditions have argued that this work is qualitatively different to that in manufacturing. The physical presence of the customer and their involvement in 'managing' the labour process; the incorporation of the way workers look and feel as a legitimate area of work, and through this as something to be managed; and the corresponding dominance of 'soft' (ascribed or social) skills all serve to differentiate service work from that with more tangible outputs.

Most of these jobs are done by women. Women make up just over half (54 per cent) of the people employed in the service sector, but 91 per cent of women in employment work in the service sector and the majority of the part-time jobs that exist are service sector jobs (ONS, 2015a), a factor which undoubtedly affects the way these jobs are structured and managed.

Emotional labour

Korczynski's (2002) features of service work included *simultaneous production and consumption* and the *inseparability* of the service process from any products exchanged. In other words, the *way* a customer is served is often as important a part of the service as the product or commodity they are served with, with different stores often offering varying kinds of service. The ambience of a restaurant and the attentiveness of the waiting staff combine with the food to make up a customer's experience of that venue. Approaches to this can vary dramatically from firm to firm.

Richer Sounds, a specialist hi-fi, home cinema and TV outlet markets itself on the knowledgeability and approachability of its staff. Customers who are baffled by the latest technological developments can come for advice on which systems best match their hopes and budgets. Aldi, a highly successful supermarket chain, deliberately employs very few staff, and instead takes a 'pile it high and sell it cheap' approach, offering (generally unbranded) goods at low prices. Any customers asking Aldi staff for advice or information about the products they sell would be likely to get very short shrift indeed. In each of these outlets staff's behaviour, the way that they work, the emotions they display and the feelings they provoke in others, are part of what is being sold and therefore a legitimate area for managers to control. When a factory worker is making widgets it really does not matter what they look like or how they feel about their work. When a sales assistant tries to persuade a customer to buy a box of chocolates, or some jewellery or a house they are expected to be persuasive, to display enthusiasm and to establish rapport. As a result managers will seek to control what employees wear, the way they look and how they feel (or at least the feelings they display), as well as what they do.

Hochschild (1983) called the way that workers were required to act out certain feelings *emotional labour*. So when a call centre worker smiles on the telephone, or a flight attendant copes serenely with the grumpiest passenger on board a plane, or a debt collector intimidates a debtor they do so not because they feel like smiling, being calm, or showing anger, rather, they do so because their employers have decided that these are the most appropriate emotional displays and that is what their job involves.

Working with emotions, particularly positive ones, can be a source of satisfaction. In Korczynski's study, when asked what the best aspects of their work were, most customer service representatives claimed that it was the people factor (2001: 93):

> When you satisfy a customer and get recognition from the customer.

> I like talking to people all day.

> The best part is the customers, the things you can do for them, rapport with them.

> One of the plusses of the job is speaking with people.

> I love what I do – working with people.

> I love this job, because I like dealing with people, resolving issues. I feel very happy when I've resolved an issue.

This is hardly surprising. Not only are most customer facing workers selected (at least in part) for their soft skills, but also interactions with customers may closely resemble those with friends with front line service workers generally expected to smile, make eye contact, create rapport and chat with customers. This can be enjoyable. After all smiling, talking and enjoying social interaction is a normal part of social life. Many customer facing staff enjoy dealing with customers, talking to them, helping them, exchanging smiles and jokes. Even the dullest and most routine of jobs can be fun. Leidner's study of McDonald's describes how workers enjoy and take pleasure in the most routine of tasks. As 'Steve' and 'Theo' comment (1993: 136):

> It's just fun, the people are fun! ... They make my day, they really do. I mean, sometimes, I can come to work – like yesterday, I wasn't really happy. I was somewhat in the middle. This guy came in, he was talking real low, and his friend said, 'Why don't you talk up?' ... I told him to turn his volume up [I laugh], and he said something ... and I just started smiling. Ever since then, I've been happy. ... The guests out here, ... they're friendly and fun. I just love to meet them, you know? I mean, it's nice working for them, it's nice serving them. Some, you know – well, I'd say one out of ten guests will probably try to give you a bad time. But the rest of them, they'll just make my day.

> Well, I enjoy working with the public, 'cause they're fun to be with. Some of them are a trip. So I enjoy it, find it very amusing.

However, as we observe below, emotional labour can also be extremely stressful. First though, we consider two other aspects of high touch service work, aesthetic labour and the presence of the customer.

Looking good and sounding right

Emotional labour is not limited to the management of feelings, staff must also look good and sound right, a development that has been called 'aesthetic labour' (Nickson et al., 2001). In the 'style' labour markets of Glasgow's trendy bars, upmarket shops and boutique hotels employees were selected on the basis of their looks. Each was expected to be 'stylish', 'tasty', 'of smart appearance', 'trendier people' or 'very well presented' (pp. 179–180). Once hired, training enhanced their natural attributes. Waiting staff in one 'boutique hotel' were given a ten-day induction in which they were aesthetically groomed. Men were taught to shave properly and women coached in how to apply make-up. All were taught about haircuts, personal style and controlling their moods, 'you have to understand what "successful" looks like ... what "confident" looks like' (p. 181). Subsequent haircuts or changes of image had to be approved by the managers and grooming was regular monitored.

The 'cast' of front line workers at Disneyland were provided with detailed aesthetic regulations that covered fingernails, teeth and jewellery (Van Maanen, 1991). Flight attendants were also expected to keep their weight below a managerially set maximum and exceeding this was a disciplinary offence (for some airlines this could be as much as ten pounds or four and a half kilos below the medically recommended weight for a particular height). Women who worked for PSA even had their bust, waist, hips and thighs measured on a regular basis. Those whose bodies ceased to conform to corporate norms were sacked (Hochschild, 1983).

It may be that some of these organisations, the up-market bars, clubs and shops of the 'style' labour market or the amusement parks at Disneyland and Disneyworld, might be considered a distinctive form of work. These are theatrical places where staff are on show, are expected to act out particular roles, model the clothing and accessories that are for sale, or simply attract more customers to drink, eat and shop at their employers' outlets through their good looks. But the management of aesthetics is not restricted to a small number of organisations. Accountancy firms provide grooming guidance to senior staff and in McDowell's research into investment banks in the City of London where high-flying employees were expected to appear 'seriously sexy in a self-confident, moneyed way' (1997: 185) her male interviewees talked of the pressure they faced to diet, exercise, dress well and exude self-confidence. This also became part of the way that senior (male) bankers managed their staff (1997: 187):

> I tell people in my team to look after themselves, sort out their BO or weight. You have got to look good.

While professional guidance (and guidance for professionals) may take the form of tips on, and expectations about, personal grooming, the appearance of lower ranking workers is often far more stringently regulated. Andy's restaurant chain in the USA insists that waitresses' uniforms must be no higher than 1–1½ inches above the knee, they are not allowed to wear elaborate make-up, or dark tights, or dark red or brown nail polish, and neither their hair roots nor their tattoos should be visible (Paules, 1991: 103). Nor is this particularly unusual. McDonald's, the Red Lobster Restaurant chain and Delta Airlines provide similar prescriptions (Hochschild, 1983; Leidner, 1996; Paules, 1991). Even where standards are not consciously set there is evidence that employees are hired, promoted, not promoted and even fired on the basis of their appearance, with bank clerks refused jobs and casino workers fired for being overweight (*HR Grapevine*, 2015; Grugulis, 2007). Significantly, reports of workers fired or not hired because of their weight are almost always about women.

Not all institutions actively manage their employees' aesthetics, and even in those that do, rules may be widely flouted with staff defiantly wearing the 'wrong' make-up, jewellery and clothing or staging 'shoe-ins' (Hochschild, 1983; Paules, 1991). But this emphasis on looks further increases the extent of the managerial prerogative, the aspects of employees that are legitimate areas for their managers to control.

Customers and customer service

The third feature of high touch service sector work is the presence of the customer. It is when customers order pizzas, buy groceries, book seats on aeroplanes or ring call centres that service work occurs. In many jobs, it is the customer who accounts for part of the variability in service sector work. Customers are part of the service process. They may have very different expectations of the process of being served, of the extent to which products and services should be tailored to them, or of the people serving them. As Leidner (1993) points out, this makes the service sector employment relationship a triangular one with features influenced, managed and occasionally resisted by customers as well as by workers and employers.

Relations in the triangle can run all ways. Employers and workers unite to face the customer, what might be described as the normal course of the service exchange. It is the employer and the employee who design and enact the workplace norms. Customer service may be tailored to particular classes of customer, as on an aeroplane where First and Business Class passengers not only enjoy different (and larger) seats than those available in Economy Class, they also receive more attentive service. Leidner's (1993) insurance salespeople were provided with scripts, which detailed their interactions with potential clients down to every last pause and joke. They welcomed these as repositories of expertise to help them increase their earnings from commission.

As well as employers and employees in alliance 'against' the customer, employers may also try to co-opt the customer in managing or rating their encounters. Almost every call centre now has an automated survey for customers afterwards in which they are encouraged to assess representatives on friendliness or warmth or efficiency. Online help will result in e-mail requests for feedback, while hotels and restaurants may have paper surveys recording each aspect of the stay. Some organisations take these very seriously. Delta Airlines included all feedback on flight attendants' files. Compliments were referred to by staff as 'orchids', complaints as 'onions' (Hochschild, 1983).

Finally, employees and customers may co-operate 'against' the employer. Paules' (1991) waitresses, who gained most of their income from tips, would often provide more generous portions of food or fail to charge for sachets of ketchup and mayonnaise in order to prompt liberal rewards from grateful customers. Elsewhere, fast food and checkout staff may leave out sections of their scripts, because they know how annoying customers find it, or, as Bolton and Boyd (2003) observed, employees may choose to engage emotionally as a gift, rather than because the rules require them to. Essentially the relationship is a complicated one, with the three parties co-operating and challenging each other. Rules set to guide the exchange may be followed or undermined, with even attempts to subvert them resulting in a better experience for some customers.

Emotional proletariat

Emotional labour, as we have seen above, is the use of emotional displays and responses as a normal part of work. Through it, emotions become a legitimate part of the wage-effort bargain; they are part of what an employee gives to their employer in return for pay. What employees look like may also be part of this exchange and the presence of customers impacts on the nature of work. So far we have considered only the positive aspects of emotional labour and the genuine pleasures that many workers report gaining from these interactions. But that is only part of the picture. After all, emotional labour does not involve redesigning work so that it becomes more pleasant, or more human, nor does it necessarily grant employees more opportunities to express their own emotions. Rather, instead of work being redesigned to suit people, people are redesigned to suit work, adjusting their emotional displays, and occasionally their emotions, to fit the requirements of the workplace.

In Marx's analysis of industrial society, the workers at the bottom of the hierarchy, who earned very little and had no control over the work that they performed were the 'proletariat'. Hochschild (1983), extending this to the service sector, argues that there is also an 'emotional proletariat' – service sector workers who are poorly paid and have no control over the work that they do but whose work involves emotions, feelings or appearance. In her study it was not the (mainly women) flight attendants but the (entirely male) 24 workers in the methods department who designed the work. They set out not only the service levels that passengers might expect, in terms of meals, drinks and snacks, but also the way that flight attendants should offer those services, smiling, meeting customers' eyes, even to the point of trying to ensure empathy with tough and demanding customers during training. Just as Marx's industrial proletariat lose control over the work of their hands, so Hochschild's emotional proletariat lose control over their feelings, the way they act out their emotions at work and their appearance. These are the fast food servers required to smile, the call centre representatives who put up with abusive and angry customers and the bookmakers' cashiers told to take bets and flirt. While the manual worker becomes alienated from their work, the service worker becomes alienated from parts of their personality, their smiles, friendliness, deference or sexuality. As Hochschild points out (1983: 198):

> [W]hen the product – the thing to be engineered, mass produced, and subjected to speed-up and slowdown – is a smile, a mood, a feeling, or a relationship, it comes to belong more to the organisation and less to the self. And so, in the country that most publicly celebrated the individual, more people privately wonder, without tracing the question to its deepest social root: What do I really feel?

The emotional proletariat is gendered, racialised and classed. The extent to which this has become a normal part of our society can be seen in an old commercial for British Airways. It showed a group of small children playing musical chairs. From their reactions it predicted what job each was best suited to. The boy who shrugged his shoulders when he lost his place would be a philosopher. The one who pushed another child out of the way so that he could sit down would be a football player. The child who carefully kept their hands on the chair seats as they walked round the circle would be a banker. The girl who stamped her foot would be an actress, and the boy who thought little of her emotional display a critic. Finally came the boy who had a major tantrum, shouting and stamping his feet when he lost a round and there was no chair for him to sit on. He would be a CEO. Seeing his reaction, a modest and quiet little girl, who kept her eyes demurely down, got off her own chair and went to the side of the room. The future CEO raced to the now empty chair and sat down, looking smugly at his fellow players. 'Some people,' said the voiceover, 'will naturally put themselves out for others'. It then went on to express the hope that 'Rebecca', the little girl who gave up her seat, would go on to work for British Airways.

It is always nice to watch children play, but the implications for adults are less endearing. In this interaction emotional expression is gendered. When the male CEO gets angry he is given a seat at the cost of another child's opportunity to play. The Rebeccas of this world, because they are naturally thoughtful, are expected to put themselves out for others time and again, and it is mainly Rebeccas, rather than Roberts, who are required to do this. Macdonald and Merrill (2009) estimate that 29 per cent of workers in the United States are employed in the emotional proletariat, but while white men are under-represented, at just under 16 per cent, women, and particularly women of colour, are over-represented, with 42 per cent of white women, 48 per cent of black women and 49 per cent of Hispanic women engaged in these jobs.

This has very serious implications. It means that nearly half of women in the workforce lose their right to emotional expression as part of that employment contract. Managing feelings has stopped being a private act for these women and has become something regulated by employers. Bolton and Boyd's study reveals the way flight attendants are treated by passengers (2003: 301):

> The passenger is 'always right'. The customer is fully aware of this and takes full advantage of the situation. They know they can say anything they want to cabin staff and get away with it, and they usually do. I have been employed as a cabin crew member for the past 21 years and I have had to suffer a range of indignant remarks and affront on a daily basis.

> As crew we encounter verbal abuse on a daily basis. Many people have no respect for crew and see them only as servants. This is shown in their manner – i.e. they expect you to carry/place bags in overhead lockers as this is 'part of our job'. They blame you for delays, the weather and other passengers not showing and holding up the flight. Many passengers are stressed before they board the aircraft. People can't ask or inquire in a pleasant manner, they 'demand'. Passengers are more aggressive as every day goes by.

As one trade unionist pointed out, if the customer is always right, those who serve them are always wrong (Eaton, 1996: 304). The emotional exchange is an asymmetric one with front line workers exempt from most considerations of courtesy or etiquette. Service workers are required to show respect, or care, or attentiveness without expecting to receive these courtesies in return. Their first names are announced by name badges and scripts, but they may not know their customers' names and the emotional outlets considered necessary for customers such as anger and abuse are denied to those that serve them. Advertising campaigns and uniforms may emphasise women workers' sexuality, so that responding flirtatiously to suggestive comments becomes part of the job. Turning emotions into commodities changes them and the conscious control of feelings in the workplace has negative, as well as positive, consequences for those who are controlled. Harvard clerical staff, upset at students' rebukes, were advised to 'think of yourself as a trash can. Take everyone's little bits of anger all day, put it inside you, and at the end of the day, just pour it into the dumpster on your way out the door' (Eaton, 1996: 296).

Even outside the most emotionally alienating occupations performed by the emotional proletariat, women workers have more, and more demanding, emotional expectations of them than their male colleagues. In Pierce's (1995) study of paralegals in a large law firm women paralegals were expected to flirt with, or mother their male bosses; male paralegals were required only to be professional and polite.

Working with emotions may also spill over into employees' private lives when they are too exhausted to engage emotionally with their partners, friends and families, or simply reluctant to carry into their homes the same smiles that they display in their workplaces. Workers can become robotic, detached, lack empathy and simply burn out emotionally. As Hochschild comments, on observing flight attendants being urged to *really smile* (1983: 5):

> Seen in one way, this is no more than delivering a service. Seen in another, it estranges workers from their own smiles and convinces customers that on-the-job behaviour is calculated. Now that advertisements, training, notions of professionalism, and dollar bills have intervened between the smiler and the smiled upon, it takes an extra effort to imagine that spontaneous warmth can exist in uniform – because companies now advertise spontaneous warmth, too.

The stress caused by these demands can be observed in the dysfunctionally high turnover figures of organisations employing the emotional proletariat. Many fast food outlets have turnover of over 100 per cent each year and Korczynski, having faithfully reported the pleasures the workers in his study got from their call centre work and their interactions with customers, noted the high turnover figures and observed that workers 'were so satisfied with the job that they were leaving in considerable numbers' (2001: 92).

Fighting back

Workers are not passive dupes in this process, nor are they automatons who simply accept management's instructions. Their responses take a number of different forms and we consider three here: humour, 'warrior service' and gift exchange. Humour, the first of these, is one way that hard pressed and put upon workers have to help them cope with the difficulties and humiliations of customer service. In the jokes and sketches on service work it is the workers who triumph, if only by answering back.

There is a great deal of high touch, service sector humour. This is hardly surprising since many of the workers in the labour market will have experienced, if only temporarily, the joys and pains of low level, customer facing work. Workers who are deprived of power over their work and told what to do, how to feel and how to look, may use humour as a coping mechanism, in which jokes become fantasies of the way they would like to behave. In the film, *Big Nothing* David Schwimmer starts work at a call centre (in the 'Steve' section, where every representative is called 'Steve', so that customers believe they are speaking to the same person each time). Here his cynical co-worker shows him how to use the mute button to make rude comments about unpleasant, overbearing or simply idiotic callers. Of course Schwimmer, on his first day, gets things terribly wrong and his vituperative anti-customer rant is heard, not only by the caller, but also by his horrified boss. In other jokes, service sector workers can really make the smart responses that they normally have to bite back. Macdonald and Sirianni start their book, *Working in the Service Society* with a joke taken from the internet (1996b: ix–x):

A single gate agent was rebooking a long line of inconvenienced travellers after the cancellation of a crowded flight. Suddenly an angry passenger pushed his way to the desk. He slapped his ticket down on the counter and said, 'I HAVE to be on this flight and it HAS to be FIRST CLASS.'

The agent replied, 'I'm sorry sir, I'll be happy to help you, but I've got to help these folks first, and I'm sure we'll be able to work something out.'

The passenger was unimpressed. He asked loudly, so that passengers behind him could hear, 'Do you have any idea who I am?'

Without hesitating, the gate agent smiled and reached for her public address microphone.

'May I have your attention please?' she began, her voice bellowing throughout the terminal. 'We have a passenger here at the gate *who does not know who he is*. If anyone can help him find his identity, please come to gate 17.

With the passengers behind him in line laughing hysterically, the man glared at the gate agent, gritted his teeth and swore, '(Expletive) you.'

Without flinching she smiled and said, 'I'm sorry sir, but you'll have to stand in line for that too.'

The man retreated as the people in the terminal applauded loudly. Although the flight was cancelled and the people were late, they were no longer angry at the airline.

Occasionally the humour can incorporate active attempts to challenge the system, rather than simple fantasies. When staff relations at British Airways were particularly poor an underground staff magazine (Grugulis and Wilkinson, 2002: 189):

aptly named *Chaos* advised on ways of maximising payments by delaying aircraft. These included throwing duvet feathers into the engine, supergluing down the toilet seat and poisoning the pilot: 'a particularly obnoxious captain can be made to suffer all the symptoms of violent food poisoning by emptying eye drops from the aircraft medical kit into his salad or drink'.

For most, however, humour provides a welcome release, an opportunity to express their feelings and give the responses they are barred from making to customers' faces.

The second way of fighting back is 'warrior service'. Greta Foff Paules (1991), in a magnificently detailed study of waitresses in a down-market American diner, argued that the waitresses saw themselves not as downtrodden emotional robots but as warrior entrepreneurs, fighting to maximise their tips. The labour market was tight, and waitresses were hard to find, so restaurant managers were unlikely to penalise them and because wages were low they relied mainly on tips for their income. To get tips they would happily hand over additional portions of food, fail to charge for various condiments and cheerfully flirt. One waitress even challenged the local drug dealers who, having sat at one of her tables to count their money, started heading to the exit without leaving a tip. According to one (1991: 150–151):

This is my motto: 'You sit in my station at Route, I'll sell you the world. I'll tell you anything you want to hear.' Last night I had this guy, wanted my phone number. He was driving me nuts. And I wasn't interested. … He goes, 'Well, how come you and your husband broke up?' I said, 'Well, he found out about my boyfriend and got mad. I don't know. I don't understand it myself.' And he started laughing. And I'm thinking, *'This is my money.* I'll tell you anything.' … I got five bucks out of him. He didn't get my phone number, but *I got my five dollar tip.* I'll sell you the world if you're in my station [emphasis added by Paules].*

These waitresses were also given detailed instructions on how to dress and how they should act; they simply ignored it and got on with working hard to secure tips.

Finally come those workers who see their service as a gift exchange, or a special emotional bond, offered freely rather than being given under orders. Bolton and Boyd's (2003) flight attendants spoke of this (just as they spoke of humour which subverted the company's rules and systems, so these responses are not mutually exclusive) and so did the nannies and au pairs Macdonald (1996) interviewed. These women were strongly attached to the children in their care and the affection they felt for them often meant that they stayed in otherwise undesirable workplaces or put up with low pay and long hours. Despite the often difficult and unpleasant aspects of their work, for these workers, emotions were given freely out of sympathy or affection.

Discussion and conclusions

It is difficult to deny the importance of the service sector to work. This is where the majority of workers are employed, so the work service sector workers do, the way they are treated and what they are paid has a significant impact on the wider economy. It is also where the majority of women work and where new jobs are created to do the work that women used to do for nothing, including cooking, cleaning and caring, as the increasing numbers of working women create a demand for this.

Service sector occupations are extremely diverse. It is here that some of the most highly skilled work is located, since the sector includes doctors, lawyers and academics. But here too, and in far greater numbers, are poorly paid and low-skilled supermarket cashiers, checkout operators, hairdressers, barristas and call centre representatives. From this variety, this chapter has focused on some very familiar high touch service sector jobs and considered the way that emotions and aesthetics

---

*Excerpt from 'Chapter 6: Resisting the Symbolism of Service' from *Dishing it Out: Power and Resistance among Waitresses in a New Jersey Restaurant* by Greta Foff Paules. Used by permission of Temple University Press. © 1991 by Temple University. All Rights Reserved.

are integrated into the employment contract, as well as the impact that customers have on and in the service process. Much of this is familiar. The smiling flight attendant, the calm family doctor and the fast food worker who wishes you a nice day are all commonplace characters in our service encounters, and the idea that service workers can and do take pleasure from their work is also one that is regularly shared. Customers can be fun, enjoyable to be with, the source of chats and jokes and even friendships.

What may be less well understood are the pressures that are on such workers, when emotions are put up for sale, when flight attendants smile for 15-hour shifts or are forced to smile at racist abuse. Turnover, a traditional and dramatic measure of dissatisfaction, in many front-line service jobs is remarkably high and workers report burnout and stress. Just as customers can provide the work's greatest pleasures, they can also be its most persistent pains, when they are rude, offensive and overbearing. Wharton (1996) argues that it is not working with emotions that has these negative effects – that actually *increases* worker satisfaction – rather it is the lack of autonomy or control over an individual's work which results in alienation and illness; a finding which has worrying implications for the emotional proletariat.

Workers have ways of fighting back, of laughing about problem customers, reshaping work so that they are warrior entrepreneurs, re-taking control of their own emotions and choosing to give or ultimately, choosing to leave. But for many, escaping from one restrictive and poorly paid service sector job, there are few options beyond another restrictive and poorly paid service sector job.

8

HRM and
the Future of Work

This book has tried to present both the good and the bad aspects of HRM, and, as you will readily appreciate from reading any of the chapters, most developments in this area can be both. Workplaces are social arenas, sites for friendships and companionship, as well as for harassment and exploitation. There is no shortage of different interests, of reasonable and unreasonable behaviour, of dramatically hyped-up new initiatives that are going to cure all organisational ills, of cock-ups, conspiracies, successes and failures. We have ways of understanding this at a theoretical level; the unitarist, pluralist and radical frames of reference which provide useful labels for the way that we (and others) interpret work, and we have also seen examples of HRM in practice in various different types of workplace. All of which are, in Hyman's (1987: 30) words, 'different routes to partial failure'. HRM, by its very nature, simply cannot succeed.

This chapter shifts our attention from what workplaces look like now, which has been what this book has dealt with, to what they might become in the future. It is a risky move since the function of most predictions seems to be to provide a source of amusement for those who come afterwards. This means that it needs to be approached with caution and that we should start by setting out *continuities* in the workplace before we start to think about changes. Many areas of working life will remain the same and some are enduring. The tensions and conflicts of interest between employer and employee are not likely to disappear any time soon because they are an intrinsic part of employment. The employment relationship will retain its partial coincidence of interest. The people in that relationship will continue to be human. Work is not going to suddenly become flawless and neither are workplaces nor workers.

So, with that in mind, we are not going to predict that the workplaces of the future will be idyllic utopias, in which all conflict has been eliminated. Conflict, in all its forms, is an inherent part of working life; it is normal and natural. That said, co-operation is also natural. Many people actively choose their job or their employer; and the daily 'busyness' of the workplace requires co-operation and negotiation on a whole range of issues. Workplaces are not battlegrounds (or not often, and not for long). So the workplace of the future is not likely to be a dysfunctional dystopia, in which there is nothing but conflict either. Both conflict and co-operation are likely to continue.

If conflict and co-operation are givens, what might change? This chapter pulls out three key features of workplaces: skills, working conditions and job security, and imagines what each might look like in the future. It is a speculative exercise, but a grounded one, in that evidence for all of these possible outcomes can be seen in the workplace today.

Let us start with an optimistic scenario of what might happen when these three elements develop in positive ways. Skills are rising against almost every indicator (Felstead et al., 2013; Green et al., 2013). More people than ever before are gaining qualifications, in both school and work, with nearly half the age cohort in the UK studying in higher education. This means that workers are more skilful, that they can contribute more to the workplace and take on more responsibilities. This could result in a grass roots skills revolution where people will 'grow' their jobs and take on more interesting and more challenging work, because they are capable of doing it.

In the optimistic scenario working conditions are also positive. Health and Safety legislation in most of the developed world means that workplaces are much safer places to be. Various forms of employment protection, including minimum wage rates, exist to protect the most vulnerable workers from exploitation. It is also possible that rising levels of skill and responsibility may persuade employers to improve working conditions yet further. More skilful and responsible jobs may pay better, and, because workers are contributing more, employers may be more likely to involve and consult them in organisational decisions. Work itself is becoming more secure, with average job tenure actually *rising* (Gregg and Gardiner, 2015).

That is one scenario, and it is the optimistic reading of some current trends in employment. The pessimistic reading is rather different. Yes, it notes, skills are rising and individuals are gaining more, and better, qualifications. However discretion is falling and for individuals to be able to grow their jobs they need discretion. Occupations such as customer services assistant in McDonald's or call centre representative are designed so they simply cannot be 'grown'. Workers do the job well when they follow the rules, read the scripts, shake the fries for exactly 30 seconds, remove the burgers and buns when the buzzers and lights tell them to and conform to the many regulations that define the job. Ironically, the rise of technology, which economists tend to link to *increases* in skills ('skill biased technological change') also makes it possible to regulate work much more closely, monitoring and measuring in ways that simply would not have been practical before and limiting the discretion workers can exercise (Grugulis, 2007). It is possible that many of the better educated young people who enter the labour market will be confined to jobs that simply cannot be 'grown'. If this is the case they are likely to be bored and alienated.

There are also worrying developments in the way people are treated at work. In the optimistic future scenario workers are treated better because they are of value to the organisation, an extension of the arguments about rationality economists tend to use. However, in real organisations, as we have seen in this book, neither rationality nor anything else can persuade some employers to treat workers well. Indeed Thompson (2003, 2011) has argued that the traditional bargain between employers and employees – that employees would give loyalty and work in exchange for security and pay – has been broken by employers who want workers who are both dependable and disposable. The bowler-hatted office workers and boiler-suited factory employees described in Chapter 5 were in a relationship with their employers which, for many (men at least), lasted for a working lifetime. Today that security is as old-fashioned as bowler hats and boiler suits and redundancy has become a common feature of working life. But it is the employers who have broken their side of the bargain, rather than the employees, with workers all too often seen as costs to be reduced rather than investments to be managed. Workers are now taking their share of the responsibility for business success and taking responsibility for their own career development. But, in return, employers are spending less on training, downsizing and putting pensions under threat.

Rewards, which are polarising now, are likely to be yet more skewed in the future. The 15-hour working week predicted by Keynes (1930/1963) depended heavily on systems for redistributing the wealth created by firms. Today this wealth is disproportionately claimed by those at the top of organisations and the rhetoric of reward incentivises the rich by giving them more and the poor by taking away even what little they have.

The process of 'financialisation', through which firms are taken over by specialist companies and stripped of their assets (Batt and Applebaum, 2010) amplifies these trends and affects job security, putting greater pressure on firms to dismiss and downsize, with redundancies used to deliver shareholder returns. In this pessimistic scenario it is also worth remembering the 'gig' economy where workers shift from project to project. As we already know, contingent work means very different things to workers at either end of the labour market. For the highly skilled and well-paid IT consultants it means increased freedom and discretion, for the low-skilled temporary workers at the other end of the pay-scale it means insecurity and financial struggles. Online jobs forums such as Amazon's Mechanical Turk and CrowdFlower take this poor pay and insecurity one stage further. These divide tasks such as data collection, classifying data, taking online surveys or transcribing into small, fractional 'jobs' and registered workers then 'bid' for work with the lowest bidder winning the auction. It is not regulated, since the forum owners strongly contest the idea that this is 'work' and the way it is set up provides no security for the workers and effectively guarantees a race to the bottom in terms of pay (Berg, 2016).

There has always been a gap between rhetoric and reality in HRM, between what employers promise, or hope to provide, and the employment practices they actually deliver. Observing this gap, noting it, criticising it and drawing out the implications for employees has long been a feature of writings on HRM. But, if Thompson is right, this disconnect between employers and employees goes one stage further than the simple disjuncture between the reality and the public relations hype we have had in the past. In this type of 'disconnected' workplace, employers view work not as a relationship, but as a series of market-like transactions and, in such a market, workers may be readily dismissed to boost bottom line figures.

It is likely that the workplaces of the future will contain elements of both of these scenarios, not least because both exist in the workplaces of the present. There will be workplaces where high levels of discretion give workers the space to 'grow' their jobs, making work more interesting and giving employers reasons to increase pay rates. But there are also sites where discretion is sharply curtailed, where jobs are scripted, intensified or simply scrapped. Workers trapped in these jobs may not be able to take on more responsibilities. Rather, they are likely to be bored and alienated. They will see their colleagues hit by the trauma of redundancy and know that they too are in the firing line. We might hope that there are more discretionary jobs than there are scripted ones, but we cannot guarantee this.

References

Arrowsmith, J., H. Nicolaisen, B. Bechter and R. Nonell. 2010. 'The management of variable pay in European banking.' *International Journal of Human Resource Management* 21(15): 2716–2740.

Arthur, J. 1994. 'Effects of human resource systems on manufacturing performance and turnover.' *Academy of Management Journal* 37(3): 670–687.

Ashton, D. 2004. 'The political economy of workplace learning.' In *Workplace Learning in Context*, edited by H. Rainbird, A. Fuller and A. Munro. London and New York: Routledge.

Atkinson, J. 1984. 'Manpower strategies for flexible organisations.' *Personnel Management* August: 28–31.

Bach, S. and Edwards, M. (eds) (2013) *Managing Human Resources*. Chichester: Wiley.

Bacon, N. 1999. 'Union de-recognition and the new human relations: a steel industry case study.' *Work, Employment and Society* 13(1): 1–17.

Bacon, N. and P. Blyton. 2003. 'Teamwork and skill trajectories: a longitudinal study of who wins, who loses.' *Human Resource Management Journal* 13(2): 13–29.

Barley, S.R. and G. Kunda. 2004. *Gurus, Hired Guns and Warm Bodies: Itinerant Experts in a Knowledge Economy*. Princeton and Oxford: Princeton University Press.

Barney, J. 1991. 'Firm resources and sustained competitive advantage.' *Journal of Management* 17(1): 99–120.

Batt, R. 2002. 'Managing customer services: human resource practices, quit rates, and sales growth.' *Academy of Management Journal* 45(3): 587–597.

Batt, R. 2004. 'Who benefits from teams? Comparing workers, supervisor and managers.' *Industrial Relations* 43(1): 183–212.

Batt, R. and E. Applebaum. 2010. 'Globalization, new financial actors, and institutional change: reflections on the legacy of LEST.' Paper to Colloquium, Université de Provence.

BBC. 2015. 'Inside Out East Midlands: Investigating Sports Direct.' 11 October.

Bebchuck, L.A. and J.M. Fried. 2004. *Pay without Performance: The Unfulfilled Promise of Executive Compensation*. Cambridge, MA: Harvard University Press.

Becker, G.S. 1964. *Human Capital: A Theoretical Analysis with Special Reference to Education*. New York: Columbia University Press.

Beer, M., B. Spector, P.R. Lawrence, D. Mills and R.E. Walton. 1984. *Managing Human Assets*. New York: Free Press.

Belanger, J., P.K. Edwards and M. Wright. 2003. 'Commitment at work and independence from management: a study of advanced teamwork.' *Work and Occupations* 30(2): 234–252.

Berg, J. 2016. 'Income security for crowd workers.' In *Precarious Work: Causes, Consequences and Counter-Measures.* Manchester: Manchester University.

Blyton, P. and P. Turnbull. 1992. 'HRM: debates, dilemmas and contradictions.' Pp. 1–15 in *Reassessing Human Resource Management*, edited by P. Blyton and P. Turnbull. London: Sage.

Blyton, P. and P. Turnbull. 1998. *The Dynamics of Employee Relations*: Basingstoke: Macmillan.

Blyton, P. and P. Turnbull. 2004. *The Dynamics of Employee Relations.* Basingstoke: Palgrave Macmillan.

Boffey, D. 2016. 'Top headhunters admit: UK bosses' pay "absurdly high".' *The Observer*: 1,8.

Bolton, S.C. and C. Boyd. 2003. 'Trolley dolly or skilled emotional manager? Moving on from Hochschild's *Managed Heart*.' *Work, Employment and Society* 17(2): 289–308.

Boselie, P., G. Dietz and C. Boon. 2005. 'Commonalities and contradictions in HRM and performance research.' *Human Resource Management Journal* 15(3): 67–94.

Boxall, P. 2003. 'HR strategy and competitive advantage in the service sector.' *Human Resource Management Journal* 13(3): 5–20.

Boxall, P. and K. Macky. 2014. 'Research and theory on high-performance work systems: progressing the high involvement stream.' *Human Resource Management Journal* 19(1): 3–23.

Boxall, P. and J. Purcell. 2011. *Strategy and Human Resource Management.* Basingstoke: Palgrave Macmillan.

Boxall, P. and J. Purcell. 2016. *Strategy and Human Resource Management.* London: Palgrave.

Brown, P., H. Lauder and D. Ashton. 2011. *The Global Auction.* Oxford: Oxford University Press.

BSAOnline. 2013. 'British Social Attitudes Survey Online.' Available at: http://www.bsa.natcen.ac.uk/.

Callaghan, G. and P. Thompson. 2002. 'We recruit attitude: the selection and shaping of routine call centre labour.' *Journal of Management Studies* 39(2): 233–254.

Cappelli, P. 1995. 'Rethinking employment.' *British Journal of Industrial Relations* 33(4): 563–602.

Card, D. and A. Krueger. 1995. *Myth and Measurement: The New Economics of the Minimum Wage.* Princeton, NJ: Princeton University Press.

Chan, J. 2013. 'A suicide survivor: the life of a Chinese worker.' *New Technology, Work and Employment* 28(2): 84–99.

Charlwood, A. 2015. 'The employee experience of high involvement management in Britain.' In *Unequal Britain at Work*, edited by A. Felstead, D. Gallie and F. Green. Oxford: Oxford University Press.

Ciujupius, Z. 2011. 'Mobile central eastern European migrants in Britain: successful European Union citizens and disadvantaged labour migrants?' *Work, Employment & Society* 25(3): 540–550.

Cockburn, C. 1983. *Brothers: Male Dominance and Technological Change.* London: Pluto Press.

Cook, H., C. Forde and R. MacKenzie. Forthcoming. 'Partnership activity as a facilitator to HRM outcomes through radical pluralism.' *Work, Employment & Society.*

Cox, A. 2000. 'The importance of employee participation in determining pay effectiveness.' *International Journal of Management Reviews* 2(4): 357–372.

Cox, A. 2005. 'The outcomes of variable pay systems: tales of multiple costs and unforseen consequences.' *International Journal of Human Resource Management* 16(8): 1475–1497.

Cully, M., S. Woodland, A. O'Reilly and G. Dix. 1999. *Britain at Work: As Depicted by the 1998 Workplace Employee Relations Survey.* London: Routledge.

Darr, A. 2002. 'The technicization of sales work: an ethnographic study in the US electronics industry.' *Work, Employment and Society* 16(1): 47–65.

Darr, A. 2004. 'The interdependence of social and technical skills in the sale of emergent technology.' In *The Skills that Matter*, edited by C. Warhurst, I. Grugulis and E. Keep. Basingstoke: Palgrave Macmillan.

DBIS. 2015. 'Department for Business Innovation and Skills Trade Union Membership 2014 Statistical Bulletin.' London: DBIS.

Deakin, S. and F. Green. 2009. 'One hundred years of equal pay legislation.' *British Journal of Industrial Relations* 47(2): 205–213.

Delaney, J. and M. Huselid. 1996. 'The impact of human resource management practices on perceptions of organizational performance.' *Academy of Management Journal* 39(4): 949–969.

Delaney, J., D. Lewin and C. Ichniowski. 1989. *Human Resource Policies and Practices in American Firms.* Washington DC: US Government Printing Office.

Delery, J.E. and J.H. Doty. 1996. 'Modes of theorizing in strategic human resource management: tests of universalistic, contingency and configurational performance predictions.' *Academy of Management Journal* 39(4): 802–835.

Dietz, G. 2004. 'Partnership and the development of trust in British workplaces.' *Human Resource Management Journal* 14(1): 5–24.

Doellgast, V. and H. Gospel. 2013. 'Outsourcing and Human Resource Management.' In *Managing Human Resources*, edited by S. Bach and M. Edwards. Chichester: Wiley.

Dundon, T. and T. Dobbins. 2015. 'Militant partnership: a radical pluralist analysis of workforce dialectics.' *Work, Employment & Society* 29(6): 912–931.

Dutton, E., C. Warhurst, C. Lloyd, S. James, J. Commander and D. Nickson. 2008. '"Just like the elves in Harry Potter": room attendants in United Kingdom hotels.' In *Low-wage Work in the United Kingdom*, edited by C. Lloyd, G. Mason and K. Mayhew. New York: Russell Sage Foundation.

Eaton, S.C. 1996. '"The customer is always interesting": unionised Harvard clericals renegotiate work relationships.' In *Working in the Service Society*, edited by C.L. Macdonald and C. Sirianni. Philadelphia: Temple University Press.

Edwards, P. 1995. 'The employment relationship.' In *Industrial Relations: Theory and Practice in Britain*, edited by P. Edwards. Oxford: Blackwell.

Edwards, P. and M. Collinson. 2002. 'Empowerment and managerial labour strategies: pragmatism regained.' *Work and Occupations* 29(3): 272–299.

Ehrenreich, B. 2006. *Bait and Switch: The Futile Pursuit of the Corporate Dream*. London: Granta Publications.

Eichenwald, K. 2012. 'Microsoft's Lost Decade.' *Vanity Fair*, August.

Ellis, V. and M. Taylor. 2010. 'Banks, bailouts and bonuses: a personal account of working in Halifax Bank of Scotland during the financial crisis.' *Work, Employment and Society* 24(4): 803–812.

Erickcek, G.A., S.N. Houseman and A.L. Kalleberg. 2003. 'The effects of temporary services and contracting out on low-skilled workers: evidence from auto suppliers, hospitals and public schools.' In *Low-Wage America: How Employers are Reshaping Opportunity in the Workplace*, edited by E. Applebaum, A. Bernhardt and R.J. Murnane. New York: Russell Sage Foundation.

Felstead, A., A. Fuller, N. Jewson, K. Kakavelakis and L. Unwin. 2007. 'Grooving to the same tunes? Learning, training and productive systems in the aerobics studio.' *Work, Employment and Society* 21(2): 189–208.

Felstead, A., D. Gallie, F. Green and H. Inanc. 2013. *Skills at Work in Britain: First Findings from the Skills and Employment Survey 2012*. London: LLAKES.

Fenton-O' Creevy, M. 1995. 'Empowerment.' In *Blackwell Encyclopaedic Dictionary of Organizational Behaviour*, edited by N. Nicholson. Cambridge, MA: Blackwell.

Forde, C. 2001. 'Temporary arrangements: the activities of temporary agencies in the UK.' *Work, Employment & Society* 15(3): 631–644.

Fox, A. 1966. *Industrial Sociology and Industrial Relations.* London: HMSO.

Fuller, A. and L. Unwin. 2004. 'Expansive learning environments: integrating organisational and personal development.' In *Workplace Learning in Context*, edited by H. Rainbird, A. Fuller and A. Munro. London and New York: Routledge.

Geary, J. 2003. 'New forms of work organisation: still limited, still controlled, but still welcome?' In *Industrial Relations: Theory and Practice*, edited by P. Edwards. Oxford: Blackwell.

Gilman, M. 2013. 'Reward management.' In *Contemporary Human Resource Management*, edited by T. Redman and A. Wilkinson. Harlow: Pearson.

Green, F. 2006. *Demanding Work: The Paradox of Job Quality in the Affluent Economy.* Princeton and Oxford: Princeton University Press.

Green, F. and D. Ashton. 1992. 'Skill shortages and skill deficiency: a critique.' *Work, Employment and Society* 6(2): 287–301.

Green, F., A. Felstead, D. Gallie and H. Inanc. 2013. 'Training in Britain: first findings from the Skills and Employment Survey 2012.' ESRC, UKCES, LLAKES, Cardiff University and Nuffield College Oxford.

Gregg, P. and L. Gardiner. 2015. *A Steady Job? The UK's Record on Labour Market Security and Stability since the Millennium.* London: Resolution Foundation.

Grugulis, I. 2003. 'The contribution of NVQs to the growth of skills in the UK.' *British Journal of Industrial Relations* 41(3): 457–475.

Grugulis, I. 2007. *Skills, Training and Human Resource Development: A Critical Text.* Basingstoke: Palgrave Macmillan.

Grugulis, I. 2014. 'Employment in service and the service sector.' In *Managing Services: Challenges and Innovation*, edited by K. Haynes and I. Grugulis. Oxford: Oxford University Press.

Grugulis, I. 2016. 'Training and development.' In *Contemporary Human Resource Management*, edited by T. Redman, A. Wilkinson, and T. Dundon. London: Thomson.

Grugulis, I. and D. Stoyanova. 2009. '"I don't know where you learn them" skills in film and TV.' Pp. 135–155 in *Creative Labour: Working in the Creative Industries*, edited by A. McKinlay and C. Smith. Houndsmills: Palgrave Macmillan.

Grugulis, I. and D. Stoyanova. 2011. 'Skill and performance.' *British Journal of Industrial Relations* 49(3): 515–536.

Grugulis, I. and D. Stoyanova. 2012. 'Social capital and networks in film and TV: jobs for the boys?' *Organization Studies* 33(10): 1311–1331.

Grugulis, I. and S. Vincent. 2005. 'Changing boundaries, shaping skills: the fragmented organisational form and employee skills.' In *Fragmenting Work: Blurring Organisational Boundaries and Disordering Hierarchies*, edited by M. Marchington, D. Grimshaw, J. Rubery and H. Willmott. Oxford: Oxford University Press.

Grugulis, I. and S. Vincent. 2009. 'Whose skill is it anyway? "Soft" skills and polarisation.' *Work, Employment and Society* 23(4): 597–615.

Grugulis, I. and A. Wilkinson. 2002. 'Managing culture at British Airways: hype, hope and reality.' *Long Range Planning* 35: 179–194.

Grugulis, I., T. Dundon and A. Wilkinson. 2000. 'Cultural control and the "culture manager": employment practices in a consultancy.' *Work, Employment and Society* 14(1): 97–116.

Grugulis, I., S. Vincent and G. Hebson. 2003. 'The rise of the "network organisation" and the decline of discretion.' *Human Resource Management Journal* 13(2): 45–59.

Grugulis, I., O. Bozkurt and J. Clegg. 2011. 'No place to hide? The realities of leadership in UK supermarkets.' Pp. 193–212 in *Retail Work*, edited by I. Grugulis and O. Bozkurt. Houndsmills: Palgrave Macmillan.

Guest, D. 1997. 'Human resource management and performance: a review and research agenda.' *International Journal of Human Resource Management* 8(3): 263–276.

Guest, D. 2011. 'Human resource management and performance: still searching for some answers.' *Human Resource Management Journal* 21(1): 3–13.

Guest, D., J. Michie, N. Conway and M. Sheehan. 2003. 'Human Resource Management and corporate performance in the UK.' *British Journal of Industrial Relations* 41(2): 291–314.

Hales, C. 2000. 'Management and empowerment programmes.' *Work, Employment and Society* 14(3): 501–519.

Handy, C. 1990. *The Age of Unreason*. London: Arrow.

Hansen, M., N. Nohria and T. Tierney. 1999. 'What's your strategy for managing knowledge?' *Harvard Business Review* 77(2): 108–116.

Harley, B., B.C. Allen and L.D. Sargeant. 2007. 'High performance work systems and employee experience of work in the service sector: the case of aged care.' *British Journal of Industrial Relations* 45(3): 607–633.

Hayes, N. and G. Walsham. 2000. 'Self enclaves, political enclaves and knowledge working.' Pp. 69–87 in *Managing Knowledge: Critical Investigations of Work and Learning*, edited by C. Prichard, R. Hull, M. Chumer and H. Willmott. Basingstoke: Macmillan.

Heery, E. 2014. 'Frames of reference and worker participation.' In *Finding a Voice at Work? New Perspectives on Employment Relations*, edited by S. Johnstone and P. Ackers. Oxford University Press: Oxford.

Herzberg, F. 1993. *Motivation to Work*. Piscataway, NJ: Transaction Publishers.

Hinsliff, G. 2009. 'I had it all but I didn't have a life.' *The Observer*, 1 November. Available at: www.theguardian.com/culture/2009/nov/01/gaby-hinsliff-quits-working-motherhood

Hochschild, A.R. 1983. *The Managed Heart: Commercialization of Human Feeling*. Berkeley: University of California Press.

Hochschild, A.R. and A. Machung. 2003. *The Second Shift*. London: Penguin Books.

HR Grapevine. 2015. 'Casino can fire waitresses for gaining weight, court rules.' Available at: www.hrgrapevine.com/markets/hr/article/2015-09-22-casino-can-fire-waitresses-for-gaining-weight-court-rules.

Huselid, M. 1995. 'The impact of Human Resource Management practices on turnover, productivity and corporate financial performance.' *Academy of Management Journal* 38(3): 635–672.

Hyman, R. 1987. 'Strategy or structure: capital, labour and control.' *Work, Employment and Society* 1(1): 25–55.

IDS. 2013. 'KFC bonuses: cash is king.' http://incomesdataresearch.co.uk/

Jenkins, J. 2015. 'The significance of grass roots organising in the garment and electrical value chains of Southern India.' In *Putting Labour in its Place*, edited by K. Newsome, P. Taylor, J. Bair and A. Rainnie. London: Palgrave Macmillan.

Johnstone, S. 2014. 'The case for workplace partnership.' In *Finding a Voice at Work? New Perspectives on Employment Relations*, edited by S. Johnstone and P. Ackers. Oxford: Oxford University Press.

Jürgens, U. and M. Krzywdzinski. 2015. 'Competence development on the shop floor and industrial upgrading: case studies of auto makers in China.' *International Journal of Human Resource Management* 26(9): 1204–1225.

Kalleberg, A.L. 2013. *Good Jobs, Bad Jobs: The Rise of Polarized and Precarious Employment Systems in the United States 1970s to 2000s*. New York, NY: Russell Sage Foundation.

Kaufman, B.E. 2015. 'The RBV theory foundation of strategic HRM: critical flaws, problems for research and practice, and an alternative economics paradigm.' *Human Resource Management Journal* 25(4): 516–540.

Keep, E. 1989. 'Corporate training strategies: the vital component?' Pp. 109–125 in *New Perspectives on Human Resource Management*, edited by J. Storey. London: Routledge.

Kelly, J. 1996. 'Union militancy and social partnership.' Pp. 77–109 in *The New Workplace and Trade Unionism*, edited by P. Ackers, C. Smith and P. Smith. London: Routledge.

Kessler, I. 2013. 'Remuneration systems.' In *Managing Human Resources*, edited by S. Bach and M.R. Edwards. Chichester: Wiley.

Keynes, J.M. 1930/1963. 'Economic possibilities for our grandchildren.' Pp. 358–373 in *Essays in Persuasion*, edited by J.M. Keynes. New York: W W Norton and Co.

Kinnie, N., S. Hutchinson and J. Purcell. 2000. 'Fun and surveillance: the paradox of high commitment management in call centres.' *International Journal of Human Resource Management* 11(5): 967–985.

Korczynski, M. 2001. 'The contradictions of service work: call centre as customer-oriented bureaucracy.' Pp. 79–101 in *Customer Service: Empowerment and Entrapment*, edited by A. Sturdy, I. Grugulis and H. Willmott. Basingstoke: Palgrave.

Korczynski, M. 2002. *Human Resource Management in Service Work*. Basingstoke: Palgrave.

Lave, J. and E. Wenger. 1991. *Situated Learning: Legitimate Peripheral Participation*. Cambridge: Cambridge University Press.

Lawler, E. 1990. *Strategic Pay: Aligning Organisational Strategies and Pay Systems*. San Francisco: Jossey-Bass.

Legge, K. 1995. *Human Resource Management, Rhetorics and Realities*. London: Macmillan.

Leidner, R. 1993. *Fast Food, Fast Talk: Service Work and the Routinizations of Everyday Life*. Berkeley and Los Angeles: University of California Press.

Leidner, R. 1996. 'Rethinking questions of control: lessons from McDonald's.' In *Working in the Service Society*, edited by C.L. Macdonald and C. Sirianni. Philadelphia: Temple University Press.

Lindley, J. 2005. 'Gender differences in job quality.' In *Unequal Britain at Work*, edited by A. Felstead, D. Gallie and F. Green. Oxford: Oxford University Press.

Lloyd, C. 2005. 'Competitive strategy and skills: working out the fit in the fitness industry.' *Human Resource Management Journal* 15(2): 15–34.

Macdonald, C.L. 1996. 'Shadow mothers: nannies, au pairs, and invisible work.' In *Working in the Service Society*, edited by C.L. Macdonald and C. Sirianni. Philadelphia: Temple University Press.

Macdonald, C.L. and D. Merrill. 2009. 'Intersectionality in the emotional proletariat.' In *Service Work: Critical Perspectives*, edited by M. Korczynski and C.L. Macdonald. New York and Abingdon: Routledge.

Macdonald, C.L. and C. Sirianni. 1996a. 'The service society and the changing experience of work.' In *Working in the Service Society*, edited by C.L. Macdonald and C. Sirianni. Philadelphia: Temple University Press.

Macdonald, C.L. and C. Sirianni. 1996b. *Working in the Service Society*. Philadelphia: Temple University Press.

MacKenzie, R. and C. Forde. 2009. 'The rhetoric of the "good worker" versus the realities of employers' use and the experiences of migrant workers.' *Work, Employment & Society* 23(1): 142–159.

Marchington, M. and I. Grugulis. 2000. '"Best practice" human resource management: perfect opportunity or dangerous illusion?' *International Journal of Human Resource Management* 11(6): 1104–1124.

Marginson, P., P.K. Edwards, R. Martin, J. Purcell and K. Sisson. 1988. *Beyond the Workplace: Managing Industrial Relations in Multi-Plant Enterprises*. Oxford: Blackwell.

Marsden, D. 2010. 'The paradox of performance related pay systems: why do we keep adopting them in the face of evidence that they fail to motivate?' In *The Paradoxes of Modernisation: Unintended Consequences of Public Policy Reform*, edited by H. Margetts, P. 6 and C. Hood. Oxford: Oxford University Press.

McBride, J. 2008. 'The limits of high performance work systems in union-ised craft-based work settings.' *New Technology, Work and Employment* 23(3): 213–228.

McDowell, L. 1997. *Capital Culture: Gender at Work in the City*. Oxford: Blackwell.

McDowell, L. 2009. *Working Bodies: Interactive Service Employment and Workplace Identities*. Chichester: Wiley-Blackwell.

McKinlay, A. 2000. 'The bearable lightness of control: organisational reflexivity and the politics of knowledge management.' Pp. 107–121 in *Managing Knowledge: Critical Investigations of Work and Learning*, edited by C. Prichard, R. Hull, M. Chumer and H. Willmott. Basingstoke: Macmillan.

Mintzberg, H. 1987. 'Crafting strategy.' *Harvard Business Review* 65(4): 65–75.

Moss, P. and C. Tilly. 2001. *Stories Employers Tell: Race, Skill and Hiring in America*. New York: Russell Sage Foundation.

Newell, S., H. Scarbrough and J. Swan. 2000. 'Intranet and knowledge management: decentred technologies and the limits of technological discourse.' In *Managing Knowledge: Critical Investigations of Work and Learning*, edited by C. Prichard, R. Hull, M. Chumer and H. Willmott. Basingstoke: Macmillan.

Nickson, D., C. Warhurst, A. Witz and A.-M. Cullen. 2001. 'The impor-tance of being aesthetic: work, employment and service organisation.' In *Customer Service: Empowerment and Entrapment*, edited by A. Sturdy, I. Grugulis and H. Willmott. Basingstoke: Palgrave.

Nonaka, I. and H. Takeuchi. 1995. *The Knowledge Creating Company: How Japanese Companies Create the Dynamics of Innovation*. New York and Oxford: Oxford University Press.

Noon, M. 1992. 'HRM: A map, model or theory?' in *Reassessing Human Resource Management*, edited by P. Blyton and P. Turnbull. London: Sage.

Noon, M. and P. Blyton. 1997. *The Realities of Work*. Basingstoke: Palgrave.

Noon, M., M. Martinez Lucio and S. Jenkins. 2000. 'Fads, techniques and control: the competing agendas of TPM and TECEX at the Royal Mail (UK).' *Journal of Managment Studies* 37(4): 499–520.

ONS. 2014. *Qualifications and Labour Market Participation in England and Wales*. London: Office of National Statistics.

ONS. 2015a. *EMP13 Employment by Industry*. London: Office for National Statistics.

ONS. 2015b. *UK Labour Market, October 2015*. London: Office for National Statistics.

Pateman, C. 1970. *Participation and Democratic Theory*. Cambridge: Cambridge University Press.

Patterson, M., M. West, R. Lawthom and S. Nickell. 1997. *The Impact of People Management Practices on Business Performance*. London: Institute of Personnel and Development.

Paules, G.F. 1991. *Dishing it Out: Power and Resistance among Waitresses in a New Jersey Restaurant*. Philadelphia: Temple University Press.

Perfect, D. 2012. 'Gender pay gaps 2012.' In Equality and Human Rights Commission briefing paper. Manchester: EHRC.

Peters, T. and R.H. Waterman. 1982. *In Search of Excellence*. London: Harper and Row.

Pfeffer, J. 1998. *The Human Equation: Building Profits by Putting People First*. Boston, MA: Harvard Business School Press.

Pierce, J.L. 1995. *Gender Trials: Emotional Lives in Contemporary Law Firms*. Berkeley: University of California Press.

Popham, P. 1992. 'Turning Japanese.' Pp. 24–30 in *The Independent Magazine*, 12 September.

Porter, M.E. 1980. *Competitive Strategies: Technologies for Analysing Industries and Firms*. New York: Free Press.

Porter, M.E. 1985. *Competitive Advantage: Creating and Sustaining Superior Performance*. New York: Free Press.

Pratchett, T. 1989. *Guards! Guards!* London: Victor Gollancz Ltd.

Purcell, J. 1979. 'A strategy for management control in industrial relations.' In *The Control of Work*, edited by J. Purcell and R. Smith. London: Macmillan.

Purcell, J. 1999. 'Best practice and best fit: chimera or cul-de-sac?' *Human Resource Management Journal* 9(3): 26–41.

Purcell, J. 2001. 'The meaning of strategy in human resource management.' In *Human Resource Management: A Critical Text*, edited by J. Storey. London: Thomson.

Purcell, K. and P. Elias. 2004. 'Higher education and gendered career development.' In *Researching Graduate Careers Seven Years On*. Bristol and Warwick: Employment Studies Research Unit, University of the West of England and Warwick Institute for Employment Research.

Ramsay, H. 1977. 'Cycles of control: worker participation in sociological and historical perspective.' *Sociology* 11: 481–506.

Redman, T., A. Wilkinson and A. Pandey. 2013. 'Downsizing.' In *Contemporary Human Resource Management: Text and Cases*, edited by T. Redman and A. Wilkinson. London and New York: Pearson.

Reich, R. 1991. *The Work of Nations: Preparing Ourselves for 21st Century Capitalism*. New York: Vintage Books.

Reskin, B.F. and P.A. Roos. 1990. *Job Queues, Gender Queues: Explaining Women's Inroads into Male Occupations*. Philadelphia: Temple University Press.

Royle, T. 2000. *Working for McDonald's in Europe: The Unequal Struggle*. London: Routledge.

Rubery, J. and P. Edwards. 2003. 'Low pay and the National Minimum Wage.' Pp. 447–469 in *Industrial Relations: Theory and Practice*, edited by P. Edwards. Oxford: Blackwell.

Rubery, J., M. Carroll, F.L. Cooke, I. Grugulis and J. Earnshaw. 2004. 'Human resource management and the permeable organisation: the case of the multi-client call centre.' *Journal of Management Studies* 41(7): 1199–1222.

Scarbrough, H. and J. Swan. 2001. 'Explaining the diffusion of knowledge management: the role of fashion.' *British Journal of Management* 12(1): 3–12.

Sisson, K. 1994. 'Personnel management: paradigms, practice and prospects.' In *Personnel Management in Britain*, edited by K. Sisson. Oxford: Blackwell.

Smith, A. 1776/1993. *The Wealth of Nations*. Oxford and New York: Oxford University Press.

Smith, C. and J. Chan. 2015. 'Working for two bosses: student interns as constrained labour in China.' *Human Relations* 68(2): 305–326.

Solow, R. 2008. 'Introduction: the United Kingdom story.' In *Low-Wage Work in the United Kingdom*, edited by C. Lloyd, G. Mason and K. Mayhew. New York: Russell Sage Foundation.

Sorge, A. and W. Streeck. 1988. 'Industrial relations and technical change: the case for an extended perspective.' In *New Technology and Industrial Relations*, edited by R. Hyman and W. Streeck. Oxford: Blackwell.

Starbuck, W. 1993. 'Keeping a butterfly and an elephant in a house of cards: the elements of exceptional success.' *Journal of Management Studies* 30(6): 885–921.

Steiger, T.L. 1993. 'Construction skill and skill construction.' *Work, Employment and Society* 7(4): 535–560.

Stevens, M. 2012. 'Employee voice has positive impact on business performance.' *People Management*.

Storey, J. 1992. *Developments in the Management of Human Resources*. Oxford: Blackwell.

Storey, J. 1995. 'Human resource management: still marching on or marching out?' In *Human Resource Management: A Critical Text*, edited by J. Storey. London and New York: Routledge.

Taylor, F.W. 1949. *Scientific Management*. London: Harper and Row.

Taylor, L. 2009. 'Thinking Allowed.' London: Radio 4.

Taylor, P. and P. Bain. 1999. 'An assembly line in the head: work and employee relations in the call centre.' *Industrial Relations Journal* 30(2): 101–117.

The Independent 1999. 'Chicony's bare minimum under government scrutiny', 29 September.

Thompson, P. 2003. 'Disconnected capitalism: or why employers can't keep their side of the bargain.' *Work, Employment and Society* 17(2): 359–378.

Thompson, P. 2011. 'The trouble with HRM.' *Human Resource Management Journal* 21(4): 355–367.

Thompson, P. and D. McHugh. 2002. *Work Organisations: A Critical Introduction*. Basingstoke: Palgrave.

Treanor, J. 2013. '200 HSBC staff paid more than £1m in 2012.' in *The Guardian*. London.

Tressell, R. 1914/1957. *The Ragged Trousered Philanthropists*. Moscow: Foreign Languages Publishing House.

Tyler, M. and A. Wilkinson. 2007. 'The tyranny of corporate slenderness: "corporate anorexia" as a metaphor for our age.' *Work, Employment & Society* 21(3): 537–549.

Van Maanen, J. 1991. 'The smile factory: work at Disneyland.' In *Reframing Organisational Culture*, edited by P. Frost, L. Moore, M. Luis, C. Lundberg and J. Martin. Thousand Oaks, California: Sage.

van Wanrooy, B., H. Bewley, A. Bryson, J. Forth, S. Freeth, L. Stokes and S. Wood. 2013. *Employment Relations in the Shadow of Recession: Findings from the 2011 Workplace Employment Relations Study*. Houndsmills: Palgrave Macmillan.

Walton, R.E. and P.R. Lawrence. 1985. *Human Resource Management: Trends and Challenges*. Boston: Harvard Business School Press.

Weeks, J. 2004. *Unpopular Culture: The Ritual of Complaint in a British Bank*. Chicago and London: University of Chicago Press.

Wharton, A.S. 1996. 'Service with a smile: understanding the consequences of emotional labour.' In *Working in the Service Society*, edited by C.L. Macdonald and C. Sirianni. Philadelphia: Temple University Press.

Whittington, R. 1996. 'Strategy as practice.' *Long Range Planning* 29(5): 731–735.

Whittington, R. 2000. *What is Strategy and Does it Matter?* London: Thomson.

Wilkinson, A., T. Dundon and M. Marchington. 2013. 'Employee involvement and voice.' In *Managing Human Resources*, edited by S. Bach and M. Edwards. Chichester: Wiley.

Willmott, H. 1993. 'Strength is ignorance; slavery is freedom: managing culture in modern organisations.' *Journal of Management Studies* 30(4): 515–552.

Wood, S. 1999. 'Human resource management and performance.' *International Journal of Management Reviews* 1(4): 367–413.

Wood, S. and M. Albanese. 1995. 'Can we speak of a high commitment management on the shop floor?' *Journal of Management Studies* 32(2): 215–247.

Woodrow, C. and D. Guest. 2014. 'When good HR gets bad results: exploring the challenge of HR implementation in the case of workplace bullying.' *Human Resource Management Journal* 24(1): 38–56.

Index